GOLF YOUR WAY

GOLF YOUR WAY

An Encyclopedia of Instruction

PHIL RITSON

WITH JOHN ANDRISANI

ILLUSTRATIONS BY KEN LEWIS
PHOTOGRAPHY BY LEONARD KAMSLER

HarperCollins*Publishers*

HarperCollins books may be purchased for educational, business, or sales promotional use. For information, please write: Special Markets Department, HarperCollins Publishers, Inc., 10 East 53rd Street, New York, NY 10022.

FIRST EDITION

Designed by Irving Perkins Associates, Inc.

Library of Congress Cataloging-in-Publication Data

Ritson, Phil.
  Golf your way : an encyclopedia of instruction / by Phil Ritson
with John Andrisani ; photographs by Leonard Kamsler ; drawings by
Ken Lewis.—1st ed.
    p.   cm.
  ISBN 0-06-016899-4
  1. Golf. I. Andrisani, John. II. Title.
GV965.R55 1992
796.352—dc20
                                                92-52562

92 93 94 95 96   PS / RRD   10 9 8 7 6 5 4 3 2 1

CONTENTS

FOREWORD *by John Andrisani* vii

INTRODUCTION *by Phil Ritson* xi

1 **THE SETUP**—*How you address the ball has a large bearing on the type of swing you make and the type of shot you hit* 1

2 **THE SWING**—*How to make a fluid start and flow into a full finish* 29

3 **THE POWER DRAW AND THE POWER FADE**— *How to cut corners on the course* 67

4 **SHORT GAME WIZARDRY**—*How to pitch, chip, and putt like a pro* 87

5 **SAND SAVES**—*Here are some proven tips on how to perform magic in sand traps* 119

6 **WINNING IN THE WIND**—*Knowing how to battle the breeze will make you a more complete player* 143

7 **BIG SHOTS**—*Once you learn these trouble shot techniques, no course situation will scare you* 161

8 **GOING STRAIGHT**—*These cures for a faulty swing will help you straighten out your crooked shots* 191

9   **DRILL TIME**—*These drills will help you practice with a purpose and play better golf*   215

10   **THE MENTAL GAME**—*Beyond grooving good swing mechanics, there's another game that must be mastered*   247

INDEX   261

FOREWORD

To equate a golf instructor with genius status seems extraordinary. But when it comes to describing world-renowned golf teacher Phil Ritson, no other word but *genius* fits.

Ritson, who currently operates state-of-the-art schools at the Windermere Golf Club in Orlando, Florida, and at Pawleys Plantation in Pawley's Island, South Carolina, served his PGA apprenticeship in his native country of South Africa. It was there that he won a number of golf tournaments, including the prestigious South African Dunlop Masters Championship. However, his true forte was—and still is—teaching golf.

In South Africa, Ritson developed a curriculum of golf education at all grade levels in the public schools, plus a national junior golf program that nurtured some of the top players in the world, including Gary Player, one of the game's all-time greats. Not surprisingly, at the young age of twenty-three, Ritson became the national golf coach of South Africa. It was then that Phil Ritson started to become a household name, both on the professional and amateur golf circuits.

Because of Ritson's reputation, Walt Disney World, which has always been bullish about golf, brought him to the United States in 1977 as its director of golf. There, at the new Florida-based golf studio he designed, Ritson taught lessons to pros and amateurs from nearly dawn to dusk. And during his four-year tenure at Disney, he compiled a comprehensive data base of information about the golf habits of the very best and worst players from around the world. It was this education that earned him such expert status in the golf world that he began to travel the globe giving teaching seminars. Everybody, it seemed—from the local club player to the leading pro—wanted a lesson from golf's new guru!

While living in England from 1978 to 1982 and working on the editorial team of the London-based *Golf Illustrated* magazine, I had heard the name Ritson mentioned over and over again. However, it wasn't until October 1982, when I returned to America to become instruction editor of *GOLF Magazine*, that I actually met the man in Florida and listened to him preach his swing philosophy to students on the practice tee. I shall never forget that day for several reasons.

Rather than teach a set method to every student, Ritson realized that each player had a different physique and possessed different strong points, so he taught each pupil differently. He was not a method teacher set in his ways.

Not only could Ritson boast superior communication skills, but his teaching language was innovative. Phrases like "try to keep the club away from the ball as long as possible" were so profound that they stimulated students and, in turn, accelerated the learning process.

Ritson's basic teaching philosophy, to "eliminate all of the unnecessary moving parts in the golf swing," brought an air of simplicity to the lesson and thus instilled confidence in the student.

Ritson had what I call "slow-motion eyes." He'd simply ask a student to swing once (a motion that takes approximately one and one-half seconds from start to finish) and he'd immediately spot the most severe fault in the student's technique almost every time.

Most of all, Ritson possessed an ultra-enthusiastic, all-knowing gleam in his eyes, common only to yogis and Tibetan monks.

Ritson has never lost that gleam in his eyes, nor his knack for spotting swing faults and correcting them, nor the art of starting players off from scratch. This is why I was honored when he asked me to collaborate with him on *Golf Your Way,* a book that we think is truly an encyclopedic A through Z guide to better golf.

Everything from how to *A*lign your body and club correctly to how to *Z*ero in on your target and hit it dead center is contained in this book. There's also a host of untold swing secrets for you to digest. So you'll have no excuse for not lowering your handicap.

Happy reading, happy golfing—the Ritson way!

John Andrisani
Orlando, Florida

INTRODUCTION

I've been teaching golf for forty-three years, and during that time I can proudly say that I've never failed to help a pupil help himself to swing the club at maximum speed and efficiency, learn a variety of new shots, master the short game, think more strategically, and shoot lower scores. Granted, sometimes it takes a little longer than I think it will for me to turn a duffer into a darn good player, or to spot and solve a subtle problem in a pro's swing. Nevertheless, in the end I always get my student to play a better, more enjoyable game of golf.

In my mind, the chief reason for my success has been a reluctance to totally become a method teacher who forces all students to swing one way, and one way alone. Rather, I decided from the onset of my teaching career to work with a student's strengths, such as exceptional eye-hand coordination, and to work around his weaknesses, such as poor flexibility, and in the process help him mold a simple, sound swinging action that stands up under pressure and lasts a lifetime.

Although I'm not a method teacher, putting some physical demands on my students cannot be avoided. Since the setup position largely determines the path and plane the club swings along, I insist that a student employ a "straight" grip and stance. Since through trial and error I have learned that right-sided swing triggers are more natural and therefore easier to employ and repeat than left-sided triggers, I insist, too, that a student start the backswing by simultaneously turning his right shoulder and hip in a clockwise direction.

Having said this, what sets me apart from method teachers is my ability to offer students choices. For example, I'll guide the pupil into the proper backswing, but let him decide whether or not it's better to stop at the three-quarter point or to swing the club to the classic parallel position at the top. Or, rather than tell him not to swing *at* the ball, I let him discover that it's best to swing *through* it—to let the ball get in the way of a good swing, so to speak.

It's these kinds of choices that stimulate the student intellectually, encourage him to experiment on the practice tee, and enable him to come to the correct conclusions about what technique works the best, according to his personal strengths and natural tendencies.

Throughout the book you now hold in your hands, I will, of course, guide you along the right road to learning the total game—from the setup to the swing, to the art of shotmaking, to short game wizardry, to the game played between your ears. However, I'll test you along the way, too. So that by the time you finish reading the clear-cut instructions and looking at the photographs and lucid, lifelike illustrations, you will be convinced that you possess all the ingredients for playing golf "your way." After that it's just a matter of practice.

Good luck on your journey.

Phil Ritson
Côte d'Azur,
France

GOLF YOUR WAY

1 THE SETUP

How you address the ball has a large bearing on the type of swing you make and the type of shot you hit

Before you start to play golf or learn to play it better, understand one fact about swing technique: *A fundamentally correct golf swing, one that allows a golfer to hit fine shots consistently and shoot low scores, emanates from a sound setup, involving the critical elements of grip, stance, posture, and aim.*

Personally, I think a correct setup position is to good golf what a mechanically sound engine is to a good ride in an automobile. Let me give you an example. Imagine you're behind the wheel of a Ferrari, anticipating the ride of your life. But when you turn the key and then put your foot to the pedal, the car chugs away like a Model T because of a minor fault under the hood. By the same token, if a naturally talented, highly coordinated athlete sets up to a golf ball with just one finger in the wrong place on the club's handle, spreads his feet too wide apart or too close together, stands too erect or bends too much from the waist, or points the clubface slightly left or right of the target, he will never employ a technically correct swing. Just as all the parts of the engine must be mechanically sound for

1

the high-performance car to purr, all of the elements of the setup, or what I call the "engine room" of the swing, must be proper and in perfect working order for the swinging action to flow smoothly on automatic pilot.

Having stated my case, let's learn how to set up to the ball like a pro, starting with how to grip the club.

The Right Grip for You: *Overlap* or *Interlock*?

If you've played golf for any length of time, you probably have read about several theories on holding the club and have also seen your high-handicap playing partners assume unorthodox grips. Therefore you've probably done so much experimenting on the practice tee and golf course that you've not yet learned and grooved a grip that promotes a good swing and ultimately straight clubface-to-ball contact at impact.

Before telling you how to place your hands on the club, I'll describe the only two basic types of grip I think you should choose

In the *overlap* grip, the right little finger overlaps the index finger of the left hand.

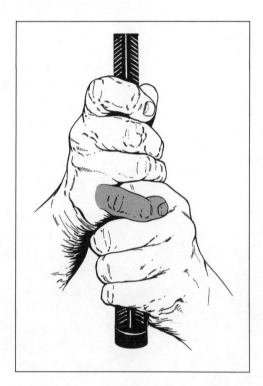

from: the *overlap* and the *interlock*. The names for these two grips focus on only one small element: Specifically, they refer to the position of the little finger of the right hand.

In the overlap grip, which I recommend for the majority of golfers, the right little finger overlaps the index finger of the left hand, either resting atop that index finger or resting between the index finger and the middle finger. The overlap grip, like the interlock, weds the hands together so there is little possibility of their pulling apart at any point during the swing, particularly at the precise moment of impact when the ball is hit.

In the interlock grip, the little finger of the right hand interlocks between the index and middle fingers of the left hand from underneath, rather than resting on top of them. I prefer to see the right little finger in the overlap position for most players, rather than the interlock. I say this because in the overlap, the right hand is in a less dominant position on the handle than the left, since the right little finger rests atop the left hand rather than on the handle itself. Thus, the right hand is a little less likely to take over and foul up the alignment of the club at impact.

For certain golfers, the interlock grip may prove beneficial. If you have fairly short, thick fingers (as two of golf's greats, Jack Nicklaus and Tom Kite, do), the interlocking position of the right little finger and the left index finger will feel a bit more secure. However, if your hands are medium to large with fingers that aren't too stubby, I'd recommend that you play with the overlap grip.

Now that you know my preference for the overlap grip with the interlock as a viable alternative for some golfers, is this preference all you need to know? Absolutely not! Many golfers seem to think that by either overlapping or interlocking their right little finger, this means that they have a correct grip. In actuality, whether you overlap or interlock is a relatively minor detail in how you grip the club. The key to a truly good grip is *the position of your hands in relation both to the club's handle and to each other.* Another major factor in gripping correctly is the degree of pressure and where you exert that pressure once you've placed your hands properly on the club. Let's look now at these vital keys to developing a topflight grip.

In the *interlock* grip, the little finger of the right hand interlocks between the index and middle fingers of the left hand.

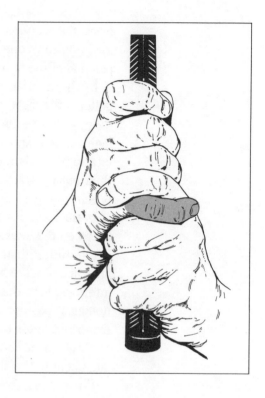

Palms Parallel at Twelve O'Clock

Whether you choose the overlap or the interlock grip, I believe that you should hold the club with the palms starting from a perfectly vertical or straight-up position, as if to point to twelve o'clock on the dial of a clock face. Just before you close your hands on the club, both palms should precisely face each other, as if you were about to clap hands.

This vertical or twelve o'clock starting position with the hands is the most natural position, since it is more or less the way your hands hang when at rest by your sides. It is also critical to assemble your grip from this starting point because it means that both palms are perfectly aligned with the leading edge of the clubface when the grip is completed. By starting to build your grip with your palms parallel at twelve o'clock, it will be far easier to return them to this position at impact. And since the leading edge of the club is perpendicular to your palms, it becomes much simpler to return the club straight to your target if you start with this palm position.

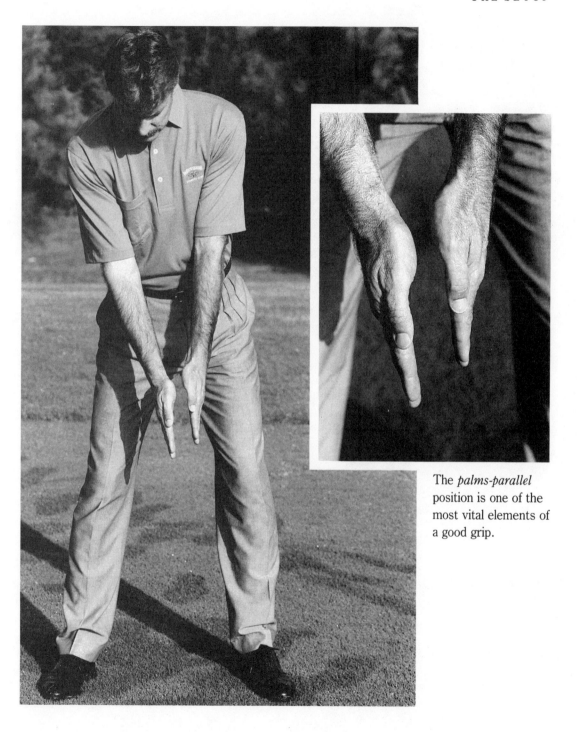

The *palms-parallel* position is one of the most vital elements of a good grip.

Build a Secure Left-Hand Hold

In formulating the left-hand grip, make sure the club lies diagonally across the roots of the fingers. This position provides the most secure hold throughout the swing, for reasons I'll now explain.

When you place your left hand on the club correctly, your fingers are underneath the grip while the heel pad of your hand squeezes down on the top of the grip. The heel pad provides you with secure control of the club and you will get the pad in this control position only if the handle lies diagonally across the roots of the fingers.

A common and serious gripping error is to close the little finger of the left hand around the very top of the grip. When you grasp the handle this way, it means the heel pad will actually be off the end of the grip, and you lose that downward pressure which secures the grip firmly against the upward pressure from your last three fingers. So make sure your little finger is one to one and one-half inches from the end of the club. This allows you to keep the heel pad in contact with the handle as well.

Now that the fingers of your left hand are securely on the club, place your left thumb slightly to the right of the top of the grip, in approximately the one o'clock position. The left-hand grip is now complete.

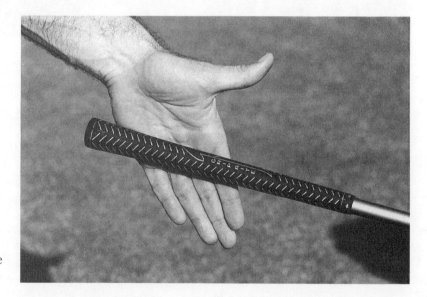

In gripping with the left hand, the club should lie *diagonally* across the roots of the fingers.

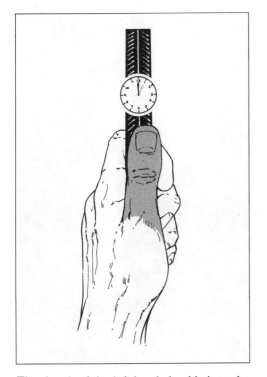

The thumb of the left hand should sit to the side of the grip; in the classic *one o'clock* position.

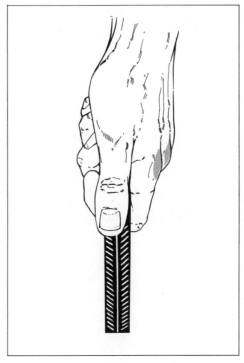

In confirming a correct grip, check that you see only the first *two* knuckles of your left hand.

There are two checkpoints to verify a correctly completed left-hand position. The first is that the V formed by your left thumb and index finger should point between your right eye and your right shoulder. The second is that as you look down, you should be able to see only the first two knuckles of your left hand.

Right-Hand Position Matches Left

Now let's place your right hand correctly on the club. With your palm flat and directly facing your target, close your fingers around the grip so that it lies directly (not diagonally) across the roots of the fingers. Be certain you don't assume a "fisty" grip with the club in the palm of your right hand. The club will never remain as secure in a palm grip as it will when held at the roots of the fingers. Also, a

In gripping with the right hand, the club should lie pretty much *directly* across the roots of the fingers.

palm grip tends to restrict the necessary hinging of the wrists during the swing.

If you are using the overlap grip, you simply overlap your right little finger over the index finger of your left hand. (I think now you can see that whether you overlap or interlock the right-hand little finger, this is only a small element in gripping the club well. It's the *positioning* of the hands and security of their hold on the club that count.)

Now you're ready to close your right hand and complete your grip. Before you do, note the "lifeline," or crease, under the thumb-pad of your right hand. A key point is to close the lifeline of your right hand directly over the top of your left thumb. There should also be a slight gap between your right index finger and your middle finger, so that it's in a sort of trigger position. This will give you an added sense of control. Finally, a V formed by your right thumb and forefinger should point up at a point midway between your right eye and right shoulder.

You have accomplished several important things by placing your hands on the club as described:

1. Both hands begin from a natural, parallel position that will be most natural to return to at impact.
2. The palms are perpendicular to the leading edge of the club-face, making it simple to return the clubface to a square position through impact, without any independent manipulation.
3. The left hand maintains a secure hold of the club's handle between the last three fingers and the heel pad.
4. The right palm fits securely over the left thumb and is also linked with the left hand via the overlap or interlock of the right little finger.
5. Both wrists are hinged at an ideal 8-degree angle.

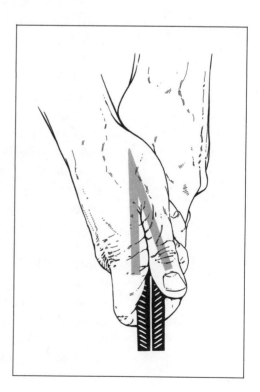

If your grip is technically sound, the *V* of the right hand will point midway between your right eye and right shoulder.

Create Correct Pressure Points

Now that your hands are placed perfectly, you are a long way toward developing a perfect grip. But you're not all the way home. You must learn to place the right amount of overall pressure on the club and to develop the correct pressure points within the overall feeling of pressure on the club.

Most golfers grip the club far more tightly than they should. This is a common yet often overlooked problem that can lead to a number of errors in the swing itself. You should never grip the club so tightly that your forearms become tense and rigid; yet this is the viselike grip pressure that's apparent in a high percentage of amateurs, particularly male players.

The golf club does not need to be strangled; it merely needs to be controlled throughout the swing. And if the hands are properly positioned, they will be able to keep control without maintaining a supertight hold at address. Try to hold the club only tightly enough so that if you were to hold the club horizontally in front of you, you could still sense the weight of the clubhead while rotating it clockwise, then counterclockwise. Another way to express the sufficient amount of pressure: Hold the club with just enough pressure so that someone who tried to pull it out of your hands would almost, but not quite, be able to do so.

Within the total pressure of the grip, there are specific points which require greater or lesser amounts of pressure. With your left hand, you should exert most of the pressure upward, with the last three fingers. This wedges the top portion of the grip securely against the heel pad. In the right hand, it's the middle two fingers that exert slightly greater pressure than the rest of the fingers.

Another point regarding grip pressure I'm often asked is, should one hand exert more pressure on the grip than the other? For all intents and purposes, the answer to this question is no. Both hands should maintain an equal, relatively light pressure on the grip, thus allowing the free swing of the forearms that is essential to building clubhead speed and squaring the clubface through impact. I will point out, though, that for people who are right-handed, the right hand will usually be a little stronger than the left. If this is true for you, it may feel as if both hands are exerting equal pressure when

To enhance clubhead control, grip more firmly with the *last three fingers* of your left hand (left) and *middle two fingers* of your right hand (below).

the hold is actually a little firmer with the right. If your right hand is stronger, I recommend that you hold the club with what feels like a very light right-hand grip. Hold the club with greater pressure in the left hand—particularly with those last three fingers.

You have now formulated the one perfect way to hold the golf club. If you stick with this grip and use it diligently both on the practice tee and on the course, before long you will see a new quality and consistency to your full shots.

I should mention here that if prior to reading this your grip position was very different from what I've described, you will have to fight your way through a period in which this grip may feel uncomfortable. How long it takes for the correct grip to become comfortable depends partly on how long you've used an incorrect grip. Mostly, it will depend on how many practice balls you hit with the new grip. So get out there and go to work on the right grip until it becomes second nature. Refer often to the illustrations and photographs in this chapter to make sure you're formulating your grip perfectly. It's a great idea during this transition period to keep an extra club in your den or living room. Practice your grip every evening while you're relaxing or watching TV. Every time you place your hands on the club correctly, you're closer to grooving it.

Don't Become a "Milkman"

You know, I see an awful lot of amateur golfers who place their hands in the desired position at address. However, as they make their other preparations for the shot, they move their hands around on the handle so much that they end up with a poor hold. I call this "milking" the grip. Usually golfers don't even consciously realize they're doing it. I suppose they do this because they are subconsciously more comfortable with the final position their hands reach before they draw the club back. Unfortunately, what is comfortable and what is correct may be two different things, particularly at the outset.

I hope making a grip change does not sound like too difficult a task. Making the change is probably a lot like giving up smoking. You know it's for your own good, so you try to do as instructed. However, it's easy to let your grip slip a bit toward your old position, just like it's easy to have "just one or two" cigarettes. Please don't fall into the bad habit of becoming a "milkman," by applying downward pressure to the grip with the left hand, instead of upward pressure. Remember that in order to hit the ball straight consistently, your palms should remain facing one another.

"Strong" and "Weak" Grips

I guess now is as good a time as any to discuss two adjectives applied so often to the grip: *strong* and *weak*. Like the words *overlap* and *interlock*, these words are used as if they refer to a golf grip in its entirety. In reality, *strong* and *weak* are just terms that describe the relative position of the hands to the grip of the club. I might add, they define positions that I do *not* advocate in gripping the club for all normal shots. But since you hear these terms so often and because they have caused so much confusion to so many golfers, let me explain what they refer to right now.

A "strong" grip position is one in which both hands are turned more to the right on the handle. Instead of starting from a position in which the palms are parallel to each other at twelve o'clock, they may be turned so that they would line up with the palms pointing to one o'clock or even to a two o'clock position. I often call this "strong" position a "Hell's Angel" grip because it resembles a motorcycle rider working the gears on the handlebars, with the back of the left hand facing upward. For many golfers, the strong grip feels more comfortable and provides a false sense of power. Don't be fooled by this. When your hands are in this position, you tend to swing the club on a faulty flat plane that causes the clubface to arrive in a "closed" position at impact—looking left of target. The result: a duck hook shot that darts left into trouble.

Alternatively, some golfers attempt to play with their palms facing too much to the left on the club, in approximately an eleven o'clock position. If your grip is too "weak"—turned too much to the left—you'll tend to swing the club on an exaggerated upright plane and usually on an out-to-in path. Therefore, at impact the clubface will be open or point right of target. The result: a sliced shot that flies right of target.

I admit it's true that a number of superior golfers, even PGA

Tour stars, have managed to develop their games with grips that are not in the neutral palms-parallel position I advocate. Lee Trevino and Paul Azinger are two examples. Both of these golf pros have won dozens of professional events playing with a strong grip. Conversely, Johnny Miller, and more recently Jose-Maria Olazabal of Spain, have won tournaments using weak grips. However, I believe these players are exceptional athletes who have been able to make just the right compensations in other parts of their swings to make up for their individualistic holds on the club. So unless you are superhuman or have hours and hours to devote to practice, follow my previous instructions for gripping correctly.

Standardize Your Stance

The second element of your preshot preparations is the development of a correct stance. For simplicity's sake, I have found it best to describe the proper stance and the correct posture (which comes next) separately. Elements of stance and posture do interrelate to some degree, but my experience with so many students over the years has proven that you are most likely to grasp all the nuances of stance and of posture if they are handled individually.

You'll go a long way toward increasing your shotmaking consistency if you make your stance automatic for all standard full-length shots. That's simple. Basically, the longer the club, the wider your stance will be. Also, realize that the ball should be played from the same position relative to your forward foot with every club.

You will assume the widest stance with your driver. Here your stance should be slightly wider than the width of your shoulders when measured from the insides of your heels. The toes of both feet should be pointed out slightly; this facilitates a free hip turn on both the backswing and the downswing. The standard ball position for the driver should be opposite your left heel. That is, if you were to draw a straight line from the ball toward you, it would point to the inside of your left heel.

There are two key reasons why I believe positioning the ball opposite the left heel is best not only for the driver, but for all full shots. First, for nearly all golfers, this is where the clubhead will

In establishing your
setup standards, know
that the driver calls for
the *widest* stance.

reach its lowest point on the downswing. Thus, you have placed the ball in the optimum position for the clubhead to be delivered powerfully into the back of the ball. Second, this position is where the clubface will reach a point precisely straight to the target line, so you have the greatest chance to hit the ball straight. This is assuming, of course, that the other elements of your setup and swinging action are correct.

While I advocate a standard ball position with all full shots from driver through wedge, understand that all shots are not hit the same way. The driver and fairway woods require a "sweeping" action, while irons require a "nipping" action.

If you're asking yourself, "How do I sweep the woods, yet hit down slightly on the irons if the ball is in the same position in the stance for all shots?" here's the answer. You adjust your weight distribution from one club to another. When setting up to play a wood shot, place about 70 percent of your weight on your right foot and 30 percent on your left foot. Encourage this by keeping your head and most of your upper body behind the ball and cant your left hip slightly toward the target.

Another factor that will promote sweep is the width of your stance. The stance is wider for the woods than for the irons, so that most of your body weight is behind the ball. This position automatically moves the lowest point in your swing back by an inch or two. Thus, you're set up to contact the ball as the driver head is just starting its upswing.

At address, you should strive to keep your left arm and the clubshaft in a virtually straight line. This is the position you should try to mirror at impact. Your right shoulder will be noticeably lower than your left at address for two reasons. First, your right hand is below your left on the grip. Second, the slightly canted left hip tends to lower the right hip and the entire right side.

Let's move on to the stance with a longer iron, say a 3-iron. The stance width for a 3-iron is about 2 inches narrower than for the driver, with the distance between the heels being just about the width of your shoulders. An important point is that you should narrow your stance by moving your right foot slightly closer to your left, while keeping the relationship of the left foot and the golf ball constant.

Your weight distribution with the 3-iron should be evenly balanced, with 50 percent of the weight on each foot. Narrowing your stance slightly accomplishes this almost automatically. Your head is still behind the ball but not quite as pronouncedly as with the driver address. This weight distribution for the 3-iron encourages you to meet the ball precisely at the bottom of the swing arc, a key to playing the long irons well. Your left arm and the clubshaft should again maintain their straight-line relationship, with the hands a touch ahead of the ball. As with the driver, maintain a straight-to-the-target alignment of the shoulders, hips, knees, and feet.

When addressing a middle-iron shot, say a 5-iron, narrow your stance to just slightly narrower than shoulder width by moving your right foot an inch or so closer to your left. For this club, move your left hip a little more to the left, so that it is just outside a straight line drawn down to your left foot. This shift places more of your total weight onto your left foot, so that 60 percent of your weight now rests on your left side. This distribution now moves the lowest point in your swing slightly in front of the ball's position opposite the left heel. If you now execute your swing mechanics correctly, you'll contact the ball first slightly on the downswing, then clip a shallow divot after the ball takes off with good backspin and control.

Again, unless you are deliberately attempting to fade or draw the ball to a tight pin position or are playing some type of trouble shot, play the 5-iron from a straight stance position as with the longer clubs.

For the short irons, say a pitching wedge shot, your stance should be narrowed about 2 more inches, again by moving your right foot in closer to your left. Additionally for the wedge, you should plant your right or rear foot perpendicular to the target line, rather than toed out as with the longer clubs. The reason for this positioning of the right foot is that it slightly restricts your hip turn away from the ball. This is desirable to increase control on shots from 120 yards and in.

In setting up to hit a full pitch shot, you'll also want to shift your left hip a little farther to the left so that you now have 70 percent of your weight on your left side. Again, the lowest point in your swing has moved forward another inch. Now, assuming you execute your swing properly, the club will strike the ball with a crisp downward blow, giving the shot plenty of backspin and control.

One other adjustment you should make for the wedge is to pull your left foot back from the target line into a slightly open position. There are two good reasons for this: First, for the shorter finesse shots, it's easier to visualize the target and get a feel for distance from the slightly open position; second, since your weight is more on your forward side, you'll more easily employ a fluid upright swing and hit crisply down and through the ball.

Develop Perfect Posture

Let's move on now to the third element of your preshot routine—your posture as you address the ball. Correct posture is often overlooked by many amateur golfers. An awkward or incorrect posture at address often proves to be the direct cause of all types of mishit shots. The reason is that if you carry yourself in a cramped posture at address or reach for the ball with your arms outstretched and tense, as so many handicap players do, you will inevitably swing the club on an incorrect path and plane.

I've often marveled at the many unusual address postures I've encountered as a teacher. My best guess is that golfers adopt them so frequently because these individualistic postures are in keeping with some very personal swing keys they believe will work magic for them. All they are doing is complicating a simple, basic issue. The correct posture is really quite simple to learn. As long as you adhere to two basic principles—comfort and balance—you will develop the right posture, and a good swing will likely emanate from it. The following tips on posture apply to every club in the bag.

You'll get the best look at a correct address posture by viewing it from behind the golfer, in what we call a *down-target view*. From this view you can see that you should be in a relaxed, yet ready position, somewhat like a basketball player getting ready to guard the opponent as he approaches.

Flexing your knees *slightly* and putting more weight on the *balls* of your feet are essential to establishing perfect posture and an on-target address position.

The first key to note about the ready position is that your weight should always be on the balls of your feet. This means your weight is centered, leaning neither on your toes nor your heels.

One postural flaw I see very frequently is that the player's weight is on the toes at address, causing him or her to lean out too far toward the ball. A smaller percentage of amateurs rest too much of their weight on their heels at address. Adopting either of these faulty address positions will lead to a poor weight-shifting action and thus plague your shotmaking performance. Therefore, to promote good balance and a smooth swinging action, set your weight on the balls of your feet. Check the weight positioning by seeing if you can wiggle your toes inside your golf shoes. If you can't, it means too much weight is on your toes.

Posture Affects Clubhead Delivery

This is a good time to clear up a misconception that many amateurs have—that both topped and fat shots are universally caused by lifting the head. How many times have you heard someone say after flubbing a shot, "I looked up," or "I didn't keep my head down"? Lifting the head may be a cause of these missed shots, but more often they are caused by changes in posture during the swing. Just as starting your swing with your weight on your toes can lead to topped shots, so also can a change in your knee flex during the swing. If you start with a nice, light knee flex at address, then lose this flex in the hitting area, as so many handicap players do, you will have raised your entire body slightly—and along with it, the clubhead. Straightening the knees during the swing is one of the primary causes of topped shots. If you're hitting the ball this way consistently, think of keeping your knees in the same flex through-out the swing as you started with at address.

The same holds true for maintaining the angle of your upper body posture throughout the swing. You should bend from the waist at address so that your spine is at about a 25-degree angle to your hips and thighs. Your butt should protrude just slightly. This angle of the spine at address establishes a proper plane for your swing. If you were to stand straight at address, your swing would revolve too much around you, as in a baseball swing. If you were to bend way over from the waist, you'd establish a straight-up or too upright swing plane.

The final point about posture is the distance you should stand from the ball. The total distance will vary from driver through wedge, but only because of the varying lengths of the clubs them-selves. Your own posture should remain constant. Let your arms hang down freely from your shoulder sockets. You should never feel any reaching, stretching, or tension in your arms at address. Simply let your arms hang straight down. Because your spine is bent forward at about 25 degrees from the waist, your arms will hang a short distance in front of your upper thighs.

Here's a good checkpoint to help you stand the proper distance from the ball no matter what club you're using. While gripping the club normally with your left hand only, clench your right fist against the inside of your right thigh, with your right thumb protruding from your fist. Your fist plus your protruded thumb should just reach from the inside of the left thigh to the butt end of the club. This amount of room is sufficient for your hands and arms to swing comfortably around your body and throughout the impact zone. You don't need to reach any farther for the ball. Doing so only hurts your chances of maintaining your balance throughout the swing.

Aim the Clubface—and Yourself!

Let's talk a bit now about the importance of aim in playing a golf course well. I'd like to draw up a scenario for you that illustrates the significance of aiming correctly, and the consequences of incorrect aiming. One or both of these aiming flaws are committed by innumerable golfers time after time—costing them an astounding number of strokes.

Suppose you step up to a par four hole that's reasonably long— say 400 yards. The hole curves or "doglegs" to the right around a large fairway bunker. Say you're an average-length hitter who can drive the ball in the 225- to 230-yard range when you make reasonably solid contact. You'd like to hit this one solidly, preferably down the middle with a slight fade to cut a little yardage off the hole. Accomplishing this might leave you in the 160-yard range from the green, which you can then hit with a middle iron.

You step up to this tee shot with your normal preparations and swing, making solid contact. Then you look up and see your ball soaring long and straight—but 25 yards to the right of the intended line, burying itself in the fairway bunker when it lands. After gouging the ball out of the bunker and scoring a double bogey, you stalk away from the green muttering to yourself, "When am I ever going to stop pushing those tee shots to the right?" To add to the injury, you may be so frustrated that on your next drive you deliberately flip the club closed with your hands through impact in an attempt to prevent hitting a "push," and hit a violent hook into the woods or worse trouble.

The shame of the scenario I've cited here is that when you drove into that right-side bunker, you may have actually hit a perfect tee shot. The only problem was, when you set up, your body and the clubface were not square to the target.

I would estimate that over half of all amateurs—and this means many millions of golfers in the United States alone—misaim the clubface or the body, or both.

From my experience on the practice tee with students, I see a slightly higher percentage of golfers aim too far right than too far left. Either way, it's a problem. And if you don't know that poor aiming is the main cause of your off-line shots, you will in all likelihood start trying to correct a nonexistent swing flaw, instead of your aim. In other words, you wind up trying to fix something that ain't broke.

Even if you aim reasonably well, it's very easy to get fooled on the golf course, particularly by a wily and clever course designer. Let's go back to the example of the 400-yard dogleg right par four with that fairway bunker guarding the corner of the dogleg. You tee your ball in the middle of the teeing area and take aim at the center of the fairway (you think), yet you knock the ball straight into the fairway bunker.

What happened? Well, you may have thought you were aiming down the middle. But you forgot to notice that the teeing area itself was pointing to the right. It's very easy to align yourself at right angles to the tee markers, and parallel to the direction in which the tee itself is pointing. Unfortunately, my friend, the course designer has tricked you by pointing the tee right where you *don't* want to hit the ball.

So before we get into your aiming mechanics, remember not to fall for this visual trick. I might add, these misleading teeing areas are even more common on more recently built courses, which usually have separate teeing areas for the different tee markers, rather than a single long strip. You may notice next time out that the different teeing areas each tend to point you a little differently. So take note of where the tee and the tee markers point, and if that's not where you want to hit your shot, make sure you don't automatically aim along with them.

Set Your Routine   I believe you'll have much greater success in developing and maintaining perfect alignment if you build a consistent routine—a *setup system* that you repeat on every full shot. It may seem to you that spending time on establishing a system of aiming yourself along with the club is a boring and perhaps unnecessary task. But aiming correctly is vitally important, as I hope the examples I've given you have proven. Remember that the person who achieves excellence in golf as well as in all walks of life is usually the one who does the little things that other people overlook. Sure you want to learn to make a great swing, and you will—but only after you've got the ability to aim that swing where you want the ball to go.

The first step to aiming well is to approach the ball from directly behind it, whether it's sitting on a tee, in the fairway, or in the rough. Stand about 10 feet, or three or four steps, behind the ball. Then draw an imaginary line from the ball to your target. Make sure your imaginary line is pointing to a very specific target. If the left side of the fairway presents the best position for your approach, draw your imaginary line there rather than to a spot down the middle. If the pin is tucked tightly behind a bunker on the right, you might decide to play the percentages and shade your approach a little left of the hole. Again, draw that imaginary line to the specific spot on the green you intend to hit.

Once you are focused on that line running from ball to specific target, pull your image back along that line and, while still standing behind the ball, pick a spot along the line that's several feet in front of the ball. This spot should be some small mark that stands out enough so you can zoom in on it—a darker or lighter patch of grass, a brown spot, a broken tee, or some other discernible mark. Once you have that spot in mind, step around to the left (assuming you're right-handed) and begin to step into your address position as follows: First, place your right foot perpendicular to your target line, at about the spot it will be in when you play the shot. As you're doing this, carefully align the bottom or leading edge of the clubface so it's pointing directly at the mark on your target line. Always get in the habit of aligning the lower or leading edge of the club at your spot, rather than the top edge of the face. The reason is that the

On all standard full shots, align your body *parallel* to the target line.

leading edge correctly represents where the clubface is pointing, while the top edge will create a distortion because of the loft on the club.

With your right foot in place and the clubface aligned, now place yourself in position by setting your left foot on the ground. For all normal full shots, your body should be aligned *parallel left* of the target line. That is, your shoulders, hips, knees, and feet should be parallel to a line that parallels the target line. This may make you think your body is aiming slightly left of the target, but it's not. Your body is lined up *parallel* to the leading edge of the clubface, which is pointing squarely at the target. If you try to actually aim your body at the target rather than parallel left of the target line, you'll actually end up aiming to the right, as so many amateurs do.

At this point in your setup routine, make some final stance adjustments, spreading your right foot back to the width required depending on the length of club you're hitting. But the alignment of your feet and the rest of your body should remain in that parallel left position. By the way, I recommend that you periodically check that your upper body is also aligned parallel left. You can do this with a friend's help on the practice tee. After assuming your stance, have your friend place a club along your shoulders, then hold the club steady while you step out of your address. The club your friend is holding should be parallel left in relation to an imaginary line running from the ball to the target.

Lay Your Right Ear on a Pillow

As you make your final adjustments before drawing the club back, you may want to look from the ball to your target and back again. As you do this, learn to get into the habit of swiveling your chin toward the target and then back to its original position at address, rather than turning your head sideways, so you do not pull your shoulders out of their parallel left alignment. I call this swiveling move of the head *laying your right ear on a pillow* because making this move is exactly the same as if you were laying the right side of your head on a soft cushion.

RITSON'S REVIEW

We have covered a lot of ground in this chapter. If you take the time to assimilate the material you've studied into your preshot routine, you will have built a strong foundation for a repeating golf swing. Let's recap the key points regarding the grip, stance, posture, and aim.

The Grip
- Overlap grip: Little finger of the right hand overlaps the index finger of the left hand.
- Interlock grip: Little finger of the right hand interlocks between index and middle fingers of the left hand.
- Club is securely gripped in the left hand, between the last three fingers and the heel pad.
- Hand relationship: Palms of hands face each other with palms perpendicular to the ground and also parallel to the clubface (twelve o'clock position).
- Thumb positions: Left thumb is at the one o'clock position on the grip, right thumb is at eleven o'clock.
- Two knuckles of the left hand should be showing on the finished grip.

The Stance
- Width of stance varies with length of club, and is controlled by widening or narrowing the position of the right foot.
- Left foot position remains constant, with the ball positioned opposite the left heel.
- Weight distribution at address varies from 30 percent on the left foot with the driver to 70 percent on the left foot with the pitching wedge.
- Hips should be canted slightly toward the target with the upper body remaining behind the ball.
- Stance opens slightly for wedge shots.

Posture
- Spine bows from the waist at approximately a 25-degree angle.
- Knees are flexed just slightly.

- Weight is on the balls of the feet for all shots.
- Hands hang straight down. Clearance between hands and body should be such that the butt of the grip is a fist-plus-extended-thumb distance from left upper thigh.

Aim

- Stand about ten feet directly behind the ball.
- Visualize your ball-to-target line.
- Align your body parallel left of your target line.
- Move your head as if laying your right ear on a pillow when finalizing your alignment.

2 | THE SWING

How to make a fluid start and flow into a full finish

One of the most common threads among all great swingers of the golf club is an uncanny ability to tie together the vital steps of the setup routine with the physical components of the swing itself. From past greats Bobby Jones and Sam Snead to present super-stars Seve Ballesteros and Payne Stewart, all sweet swingers share a waltzlike gracefulness that starts the second they pull the club out of the bag, and ends the moment they finish their swing. Every individual movement flows into the other; and because of this carefully choreographed process of blending the setup with the swing, the typical tour pro's swinging action looks effortless, yet it produces very powerful, very accurate shots.

By contrast, most club-level amateur golfers do not exhibit this relaxed wholeness that connects the fundamental steps of the setup with the vital movements in the swing. Frankly, in observing thousands of pupils, both on the practice tee and out on the golf course during playing lessons, I've noticed that often the typical amateur starts out assessing the shot in a super-relaxed fashion. However, by the time he steps up to the ball and prepares to take the club back, he freezes—then yanks the club back very quickly and on an incorrect path. The result: a mishit. For this reason particularly, I'd like to explain the "waggle" before discussing the "guts" of golf swing mechanics, because this pressing movement is a vital step in bridging the gap between the setup and the swing.

The Waggle: A Miniature Swing

The way a golfer waggles the club (waves the clubhead away from the ball a few times before he swings) is usually a precursor to the tempo and rhythm, and even the positioning, of the club during the swing itself. Show me a golfer with a quick, jerky, hand- and wrist-dominated waggle in which the clubhead jumps around violently, and I'll show you a golfer with an erratic golf swing. On the other hand, if a player makes smooth, rhythmic movements of the clubhead, chances are the swing that flows out of the waggle will display good control.

There's no *one* set way to waggle the club, because every golfer has his own natural swing tempo. Furthermore, the waggle is pretty much instinctual and geared to a golfer's personal way of swinging. Having said that, I want to emphasize that no matter how personalized the waggle is, certain fundamentals must be followed for it to trigger a technically sound swing.

First, the waggle should be a very brief and very gentle movement, directed mostly by the arms, but involving a touch of wrist action, too. Second, the clubhead should travel back from the ball only a short distance, not more than 12 inches. Third, the clubhead should pretty much travel along the target line throughout the motion or else you'll be susceptible to swinging on an incorrect plane.

Next time you're watching a golf tournament on television, take note of the preswing waggles employed by the pros. Most top players exhibit very soft, finely controlled waggles. Tom Kite's waggle is excellent, because it's really an exact miniature of the smoothly paced, relatively wide arc he creates during the actual swing. Ray Floyd is another player with an excellent waggle that is congruent with his own somewhat unique, but very effective, swing. Floyd makes clockwise circular movements of the clubhead

The way you *waggle* the club has a whole lot to do with the way you swing it.

behind the ball, prepping himself for his own flatter takeaway action. It doesn't really matter which player you watch. What matters is this: After a certain number of waggles—it could be one, it could be twenty—watch how each pro puts his swing in the "go" mode. Of course, exactly when he stops waggling and starts to flow into the first movement of the swing (the takeaway) is a personal preference having to do practically entirely with individual "feel."

The Takeaway: Body and Hands Turn Together

Many amateurs who come to me for lessons have been told by previous teachers to keep the clubface on the target line for as long as possible during the takeaway. Not only is this a forced, unnatural position for a player to employ, but it can lead to major problems later in the swing. The clubface should never remain exactly straight, or square, to your target line throughout the takeaway or during the swing. Nor should it remain straight in relation to the target during the takeaway. Rather, the clubface remains straight in relation to the natural path of the clubhead along the entire plane of the golf swing. This means that when the clubface has moved, say, 18 inches back from the ball, it will be looking a touch to the right of the target line—while remaining straight in relation to the *path* of the swing, which has begun to move slightly inside the target line.

Here is a simple test to see if you're making a natural, straight takeaway:

1. Set a wooden two-by-four just outside the target line and parallel to it.
2. Set up as you normally would, placing the toe of the club against the side of the board at address.
3. Make a slow-motion full-body takeaway.
4. Observe the clubhead. You'll notice that after it's moved back only a few inches, the toe of the club will no longer be touching the board; that is, it will have moved slightly inside the target line. The clubhead should gradually continue to move more inside the target line the farther you swing it back.

Again, I do *not* recommend that you try to keep the clubhead on the target line during the takeaway. This is an unnatural move that almost always leads to a faulty "flying" right elbow position at the top of your swing. I might also add that you should *not* strive to keep the clubhead low to the ground for any extended distance during the takeaway. While I don't advocate picking the club up with

In the takeaway, the clubhead travels along a path, slightly *inside* the target line.

the hands and wrists, you'll see that a natural, right-sided movement involving the right hand, arm, shoulder, and hip will draw the clubhead very gradually up and away from the ground as well as inside the target line. Trust the movement of your entire right side to take the club back and don't force it to do anything else.

Develop Rotation Power in Your Backswing

At this point, I'd like to introduce a key term that I'll repeat often in describing both the correct backswing and correct downswing movements. This term is *rotation power.* Rotation power refers to the use of the large muscles of the right side to create leverage in the backswing. Then, rotation power from your left side pulls and ultimately releases that pent-up leverage during the downswing, transferring astonishing speed and power to the clubhead as it flashes through the impact zone.

I believe you will find it far easier and more natural to continue to use the large muscles of your right side to bring the club all the way up to the top of your backswing. There are more nerve endings or "frequencies" in your smaller muscles than in your larger muscle groups. This means that if you rely on your hands and wrists to control the backswing, it is unlikely that you'll move the clubhead on the correct path and plane consistently. You also don't achieve nearly the windup with a hands-oriented backswing as you do when utilizing the whole right side. For these reasons, I advise you to keep your hands and wrists quiet throughout the entire backswing action. By quiet, I mean that they should remain in the same position relative to your arms that they were in at address, and should take no action on their own.

Let's take some time to study the precise role of the body in developing backswing rotation power. As your right hip is turning in a clockwise direction and your right arm and shoulder are carrying the club back, your weight should begin to rotate and shift onto your right knee and right heel. By the time you reach the top of the backswing, about 80 percent of your weight should be channeled here.

The right knee is a very important element to a sound backswing; you must keep it in its original position throughout the backswing as it accepts the weight shift. There's a very strong tendency to let the right knee buckle outward—that is, to the right. This causes excessive lateral upper body and head movement; in turn, this sway prevents you from returning the club squarely into the ball. However, if the right knee stays firmly flexed, your head and upper body will remain quiet as well. You'll know you're on the

During the early stage
of the backswing, the
hands and wrists must
stay *quiet*.

right track if, when you swing back, you feel pressure on the inside
of your right knee joint.

As the right side swings the club back, your right elbow should
be angled toward your left elbow, in the classic "tray" position.
Winging the elbow far away from the body indicates that your arms
are overcontrolling the action. At the same time, you are lifting the
club well above the desired natural swing plane produced by a good
body turn.

Maintaining the flex in the *right* knee is critical to employing a sound backswing motion.

We have not talked specifically about the shoulders as yet. Of course, they also play a very significant role in developing a powerful coil. Your shoulders should always turn at an angle that is perpendicular to your spine. That is, the turn is at right angles to the 25-degree angle of bend from the waist that you set for your spine at address.

To give you the proper image of the movement of the shoulders during the backswing, think of them acting like a seesaw. At address, your shoulders will be like a seesaw that is more or less parallel to the ground. On the backswing your right shoulder should move up as well as around. Your left shoulder, meanwhile, should move down and under your chin, acting like the lower half of the seesaw.

Once you learn to use the full-body takeaway and backswing action, you'll find that your shoulders turn *automatically*, remaining perpendicular to your spine.

With regard to how far you should turn your shoulders as well as your hips on the backswing, there is no set amount of turn that's right for everyone. The degree of turn depends on each player's individual flexibility of the hips, torso, and shoulders. Since turning power produces powerfully accurate shots, I do, however, urge every golfer to make as full and aggressive a turn as possible, while keeping his weight on the right knee and right heel. Ideally, your shoulders should turn about 100 degrees away from the ball, with your hips turning about 55 degrees, while the top of your left arm stays closely connected to your body.

Two Key Answers to Two Key Questions About the Backswing

There are two questions regarding the backswing movement that my students constantly ask me. The first is, "How long should my backswing be?" My answer is that there *is* no set answer to this question. The length of every golfer's backswing will vary in relation to the fullness of his or her hip turn. Very flexible players may swing the clubshaft to a point beyond parallel to the ground. If they can do this while keeping their weight on the inside of the right heel and with the left arm and hand retaining firm control of the club, then it's perfectly all right if the clubshaft reaches a point where it is past parallel. Incidentally, I find that women golfers, generally being more flexible and less muscular than men, are usually able to make a relatively long backswing while remaining in control of the club.

The reality, though, is that most golfers cannot swing beyond parallel and still control both the club and their weight shift. Some

On the backswing, the right shoulder should move *up* as well as around, while the left shoulder moves *down* and under your chin.

Since a powerful coiling action helps produce a powerful shot, turn the shoulders as *fully* as possible.

amateurs may reach the classic parallel position, but the majority will find that the club moves back only to a three-quarter position— one in which the clubshaft is about halfway between perpendicular and parallel to the ground. I strongly believe that a three-quarter position is also perfectly fine, as long as you are coiling as fully as possible while maintaining control of your body and the club. There is no need to manufacture an artificially long backswing by bending the left elbow sharply at the top of the swing, one very common swing flaw that actually robs you of both power and control.

I believe the whole issue of backswing length is highly overrated. If you maintain control of the club while making as full a backswing turn as you are capable of, you can obtain excellent distance even from a three-quarter backswing position.

To convince yourself that a big swing isn't always better, look at Jack Nicklaus, who just so happens to be the greatest player in golf history. Today, well into his fifties, Nicklaus is not nearly as supple as he was during his early pro days. Owing to this loss of flexibility and an on-off back problem, his driver swing now stops well short of parallel (and many of his iron shot swings do not even reach the three-quarter position). Yet the amazing fact is that Nicklaus hits the ball nearly as far off the tee as he did in his heyday. So it's not the length of the backswing that counts, but rather how well you develop rotation power by winding your big muscles.

The second question students frequently ask is, "Should I lift my left heel on the backswing?" Like the question of how long your backswing should be, whether or not you should let your left heel lift is a question that must be answered individually. Again, it all depends on the suppleness of your physique. Some players can make a full, powerful turn of the shoulders and hips while keeping their left heel on the ground, or just slightly raised. Among the PGA Tour stars, Greg Norman and Tom Purtzer are two very strong hitters who can keep the left heel very close to the ground throughout the backswing.

I feel that many golfers, particularly amateurs who may not be in their best athletic condition, will find that when they make a full shoulder and hip turn, the force of this turn will pull the left heel 2 inches or more off the ground. As long as you're keeping your weight firmly planted on the inside of your right heel at the top of the backswing, I see nothing wrong with letting your left heel rise. Again, the greatest example of a player whose left heel rises noticeably on the driver swing is Jack Nicklaus. Obviously this move has proven very acceptable, as Jack's twenty major championship titles attest!

As long as you are building your rotation power to the maximum within the framework of good balance throughout the swing, how far your left heel rises is not a crucial point. Let it lift the amount that's natural for you. My only warnings are these: Never consciously raise the left heel in an artificial attempt to help you make a weight shift as a substitute for developing a full-body turn. And, conversely, never force your left heel to stay down if it wants to be pulled up by the coiling of your backswing, as this will severely limit your turn and thus your rotation power.

Whether or not you should allow the left heel to *lift* is simply a matter of personal preference.

Left Arm "Soft"   If you make the proper right-sided backswing movements as described, the left arm should correctly bend, just slightly, as you reach the top of your swing. Let's analyze its position more closely, however, since it's so vital to the outcome of the shot.

I believe in what I call a "soft" rather than a very firm left arm at the top of the backswing. While you may have heard advice that you should keep the left arm as straight as a yardstick as you reach the top in order to keep a perfect radius for the arc of the swing, I don't quite agree with this theory. I find that golfers who strive for a ramrod-straight left arm tend to restrict the flow of their swings heading into that crucial transition from backswing to downswing. Therefore, the very firm left arm often costs them more than it helps them.

Instead, allow for a little "softness" in the left arm. Don't consciously bend it, of course. But you may find that the weight of the clubhead at the top of the swing may naturally encourage the slightest of bends in the left elbow. If so, that's fine. Don't fight it; otherwise you'll likely disrupt the flow of your swing. Remember that *you want the golf swing to be one continuous motion from start to finish, rather than just a set of mechanical positions to strive for.*

While your left arm may give a little, your left wrist, meanwhile, should maintain the same relationship to the back of your left arm at the top of the swing that it did during the address.

This constant left wrist angle acts as a steering wheel for your shots because the clubface will follow or match the position of your left wrist. Maintain the angle of the left wrist at the top and you'll find it much easier to deliver the clubface squarely into the ball at impact. Periodically, then, it's a good idea to have a friend check to see if at the top of the backswing your left wrist is flat and your right wrist flexed back, just as they were at address.

While the left wrist remains in its proper position as you reach the top, there *will* naturally be a gradual setting of the wrists. This setting or cocking of both wrists will occur very naturally in response to the weight of the clubhead, just as that weight may cause the left elbow to give slightly. I want to make sure here that you understand the following points: First, this wrist set is a vertical

A little *bend* in the left arm on the backswing is perfectly permissible.

At the top of the swing, your left hand, wrist, and forearm must maintain the *angle* first established at address.

hinging rather than a side-to-side flipping of the wrists; second, the wrist setting is a natural process that occurs as the clubhead swings back. I do *not* agree with those who advocate a contrived, exaggerated setting of the wrists, as this robs you of the width of clubhead arc, which is an important factor in developing power.

Ideally, at the top of your backswing the clubshaft should be parallel to the target line. If you are keeping your right elbow angled toward your left elbow, your right wrist flexed back, and your left wrist straight, the chances are good that your clubhead will be correctly positioned. Again, have a friend stand behind you to check this clubshaft alignment and make sure you're on track.

An "In-Motion" Transition

You have reached the top of the backswing while making an excellent body coil and with the club nicely on plane. This is the point in the swing which raises another question for many of my students—namely, "Should I pause at the top of the backswing?"

I believe the body should always remain in motion during the golf swing. Which is to say: No, there should be no distinct pause at the top of the swing. Stop and think about it. If you needed to pause, then you really wouldn't need to make a golf swing as we know it. You could just manually place the club up there where you thought you wanted it, then swing the club down from the top. But believe me, this "downswing only" method would not be nearly as effective as a true, start-to-finish golf swing.

The fact is that, in an excellent transition from backswing into downswing, it is only an illusion that the club has paused at the top. That's because in a good golf swing, your body will actually be moving in two directions *simultaneously* at the top of the swing. While your upper torso is completing its windup away from the target, your left knee should already be starting to unwind in the direction of the target. This simultaneous movement in two directions may actually freeze the clubshaft in place for the slightest instant—hence the appearance of a pause at the top.

As I stated earlier, golf played at its best is a two-sided game. It is the movement of the left knee during the swing's transition that begins the left side's dominance during the second half of the swing.

As you shift your left knee toward the target, the legs actually separate a little farther apart. This leg separation is the beginning of the creation of the leverage on the downswing that will allow you to strike the ball with more power than you ever dreamed of. So even as you feel your upper body concluding its turn to the right, start the transition by shifting your left knee toward the target.

The Downswing: Keep the Clubhead "Away" from the Ball

Your left knee has started a chain reaction in which your entire left side takes control of the downswing. This is crucial because it means that your left side will be pulling the club through the downswing, just as the right side did the pulling while the club was moving in the opposite direction. And, as you probably remember from your physics classes, any pulling action on an object (in this case, the golf club) is more efficient than a pushing action. This simple law explains why *the right-side-controlled backswing and left-side-controlled downswing—both pulling actions—provide by far the most efficient overall golf swing.*

But back to the start of the downswing. Once you have shifted your left knee in the direction of the target, your next key move is to turn your left hip and side in counterclockwise fashion, to your left and rear. This move immediately shifts most of your weight back onto your left foot and sets up the proper chain action in which the pent-up speed of the clubhead will be released at the very last instant.

I'd like to reiterate right here that letting the right side dominate the start of the downswing will almost certainly destroy your golf swing, or at least markedly diminish its effectiveness. Any attempt to hit *at* the ball with your right shoulder, arm, and/or hand will throw the club outside the plane you swung the club back on, and also outside the target line. This damaging over-the-top move also causes the clubhead to come into the impact zone at an undesirable steep angle. The end result of right-side domination for most amateurs is the dreaded slice.

Here are two key thoughts that I have found have really helped my students make good use of their left sides while keeping their right sides from taking over the downswing: *Retain the pressure in*

As your left knee rotates toward the target, your legs should *separate*.

Rotating your left hip
in a *counterclockwise*
direction ("clearing" it)
ensures a proper
weight shift.

*your right knee and try to keep the clubhead away from the ball for as
long as possible on the downswing.* "Why should I try to keep the
clubhead away from the ball? I eventually have to hit it, don't I?"
you might reasonably ask. And my answer is: Yes, eventually the
clubface will strike the ball. However, by thinking of keeping the

Turning your body through the shot allows you to deliver the club *squarely* into the ball.

clubhead away from the ball in the downswing, what is it that you are actually doing? You are keeping your hands, arms, and right shoulder back, rather than bringing them closer to the ball with that swing-wrecking over-the-top move, called the "early hit."

You don't need to do anything with your hands and wrists to

propel the club into the ball. Simply continue your downswing by turning your body through the shot, keying on your left hip and side. Do not make any attempt whatsoever to hit at the shot with your right side, in effect bringing your hands—and the clubhead— closer to the ball. The rotary turn of your hips will automatically bring your hands, arms, and the clubhead out and around so that the clubhead returns to the back of the ball on a relatively shallow path, from inside to along the target line at impact. You do not have to do anything with your right side to help the clubhead get there.

Here is another swing thought to help you make a good, left-sided, pulling action on the downswing: Keep the upper part of your left arm fairly close in to your chest through impact. By accomplishing this, you'll find it's virtually impossible to throw the clubhead outside the target line with your right side.

So, for a controlled, power-producing downswing, focus on an initial left knee slide toward the target, followed by a strong left-side rotation with the weight moving smoothly from the little toe of the left foot to the outside of it. And make sure to keep that clubhead away from the ball for as long as possible.

Keys to Solid Impact

By the time you have reached the impact zone, you will have rotated at least 80 percent of your weight onto the outside of your left foot. The remaining weight will be on the inside of your right foot, while the right heel is being pulled off the ground by the force of the swing. Meanwhile, your head should remain steady behind the ball.

There is one very important key to my system for obtaining maximum clubhead speed and consistency at impact. That is, at impact, your left wrist should be perfectly straight, while your right wrist remains in the slightly flexed-back position you started in at address. This is a key that you will see repeated several times throughout this book.

You see, by striving to keep the right wrist flexed back through the impact zone, you will be accomplishing something that's very important to making pure contact. It means you are keeping the right hand from prematurely flipping the clubhead off line, and also

Keeping the upper
part of your left arm
fairly *close* to your
chest helps you hit
powerfully through the
ball.

retaining the clubhead's maximum speed until the last possible
instant.

   I cannot be too emphatic on this point: For any normal full shot,
you must not make any conscious effort to hit or add power to the
shot through impact. Any attempt to hit with your hands will only
serve to throw away clubhead speed prematurely, as well as increase the chance of delivering the clubhead inaccurately to the ball
and mishitting the shot.

   Please, trust the concept of the rotation power generated by your body turn, and the centrifugal force it generates through impact. I have worked with many students whose full swings have previously been ineffective because they swing with their hands and wrists, not with their bodies. Often it takes some time before they're convinced to activate their bodies while pacifying their hands through impact. Once they grasp this concept, however, the results are often downright amazing. Trust the rotation power you've developed to transmit power through your hands.

Let Your Head Go with the Shot

One of the oldest maxims of golf instruction is that you must keep your head still throughout the golf swing. While I agree that it's fine if you actually do keep it reasonably still, too much emphasis has been placed on this tenet. From observing the finest professionals along with many top amateurs, it's fairly obvious that for most, head movement does occur during the follow-through. And as long as this movement is limited to an inch or so, I don't believe it's necessarily a bad thing.

The swings of the best players exhibit free-flowing movement both in the backswing turn and in the downswing and follow-through. With this rotary body movement, oftentimes a touch of lateral head movement may also take place. That is, the head may move about an inch to the right, away from the target, on the backswing, then move laterally back to its original position during the downswing and impact.

Note that when I say a minimal amount of head movement is okay, I'm referring to a slight lateral or side-to-side movement. There is no room for any vertical, up-and-down bobbing of the head in the golf swing. And the fine rotary golf swing's movements will never be the cause of this fault.

I believe that if you make keeping your head precisely in place your number one priority throughout the swing, you'll end up restricting your swing motion and fail to develop the necessary body rotation needed for long, straight shots.

Through the impact zone, I don't believe you should keep your head down in a static, rigid position. This is because keeping your head down rigidly restricts the free-swinging motion of your upper body through the ball. You could easily wind up hitting at the ball rather than swinging right *through* it. Also, straining to keep your head rooted past impact can lead to neck strains, and possibly more severe injuries.

On the downswing, remember the movement of your shoulders in seesaw fashion. The turning of the shoulders through the downswing, perpendicular to your spine, brings the right shoulder down, under your chin, while the left shoulder works back up. However, instead of forcing your head to stay down as the right shoulder moves past it, it's much better to let your head rotate slightly clockwise, swiveling along with your shoulders through the impact zone and into the follow-through. The result will be a much smoother move through the hitting area, and, to boot, you'll probably avoid a "pain in the neck" at some time in the future.

Extend Right Arm into Follow-Through

As the club moves through the impact zone, there's one technical point involving the arms that often goes unnoticed, but which I have found very significant in my teaching.

I find that many, if not most, right-handed amateurs have a tendency to force the left arm to remain straight through impact. By keeping the left arm straight longer than it should remain so, the player is actually preventing his right arm from making a free release through the ball. This costs him or her a tremendous amount of acceleration, and thus power and accuracy as well. An untold number of golf shots have been mishit because the right arm was never extended fully and the player was trying to "find" the ball with the clubhead.

Remember that in many ways golf really is a game of opposites. And this tenet is supported by the opposing left arm–right arm relationships during the backswing and downswing. Just as the right arm folds while the left stays relatively firm in the backswing, so must the left arm fold while the right arm extends fully through impact in order to maintain a consistently flowing arc through the completion of the swing.

Point Your Navel to the Target

I have found time and again during my teaching that a great image is worth a thousand words—maybe more! And I have just the image that will help you move vigorously through impact and up into a full, balanced, graceful follow-through.

The image is, point your navel or belly button at the target.

By finishing with your navel toward the target, you're assuring yourself that you have applied a full rotation of your left side (and the right side following it) through the ball, so that the clubface is automatically squared up at impact without the need for any independent hand or wrist manipulation. Finishing with the navel at the target also guarantees a well-balanced follow-through, with the shoulders level to the ground, your weight almost entirely on the outside of your left foot, and your arms and the club held over your left shoulder in a relaxed position.

Conversely, you can tell that the player who finishes with the navel pointing closer to the ball's original position than to the target has not really utilized the left hip and side to develop downswing power. Instead, this player has more or less waved at the ball with the arms and hands, while the midsection has remained static.

So point your navel at the target for a full, powerful, body-oriented movement through the shot.

Here is a finishing touch to developing a perfect follow-through: Practice *posing for a camera* at the completion of the swing. As the ball soars high and straight toward the target, indulge yourself by holding your finish for 3 or 4 seconds as you enjoy its perfect flight. It's a good sign if you can hold this pose, too. It indicates perfect balance, and perfect balance in the follow-through can emanate only from a sound, well-balanced backswing and downswing motion.

These, then, are the basics to developing a sound, repeating, continuous swing action. Like anything else that is of value, ingraining these fundamentals will take some time and effort. Particularly if what you have read here indicates that you need to implement quite a few changes in your swing, I strongly recommend that you

If you can easily hold a high *finish* position for a few seconds, you probably employed a sound swing.

practice even more than you play for a while, until the "feels" of the entire action we've discussed start to become second nature.

Whatever your handicap level, I promise you that by following this swing system religiously, you will begin to see improvement in your long game. And it will happen much faster than you think.

With that, let's review the fundamentals of the powerful, repeatable golf swing, in the order in which they occur.

RITSON'S REVIEW

The Waggle
- The waggle sets the tempo for the swing that follows.
- Move the club along the path you plan for the takeaway, using your arms with a slight bit of hand and wrist action.

The Takeaway
- The takeaway emanates from the waggle with no discernible stop in the action.
- Use your entire right side to draw the club away from the ball.
- Keep the clubface straight in relation to the path of the swing.
- Test your takeaway path against a two-by-four.

The Backswing
- Develop rotation power by using the large muscles of the right side.
- Shift your weight onto your right knee and right heel.
- Turn the shoulders perpendicular to the angle of your spine.
- Strive for as full a shoulder and hip turn as possible.
- Let the wrists set naturally.
- Keep the left arm soft, left and right wrists straight.

Transition and Downswing
- Move your left knee down an imaginary line running along your feet.
- Shift your left hip around to the left.
- Keep your right shoulder and arm passive throughout the downswing.
- Keep the clubhead away from the ball as long as possible.
- Keep the upper part of your left arm in close to your chest.
- Retain pressure in your right knee.

Impact Zone
- Shift 80 percent of your weight onto the outside of your left foot.
- Keep your right wrist bent back, in a "straight" position.

- Let rotation power release the clubhead freely through the ball.
- Let your head release with the upper body through the shot.

Follow-Through
- Let the follow-through be a one-piece movement, involving *both* sides of the body.
- Allow your left arm to fold as your right arm extends.
- Nearly 90 percent of your weight should be on your left foot.
- Finish with your navel facing the target.
- Pose as if for a camera.

Position One

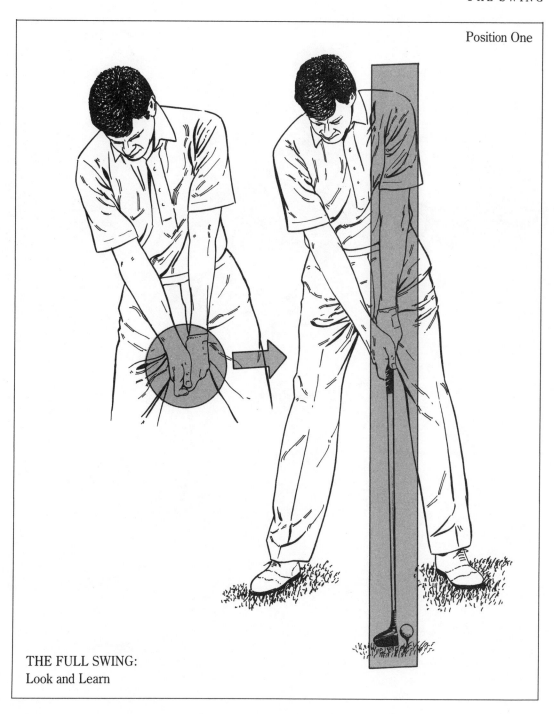

THE FULL SWING:
Look and Learn

Position Two

Position Three

Position Four

Position Five

Position Six

Position Seven

3

THE POWER DRAW AND THE POWER FADE

How to cut corners on the course

One of the beauties and mysteries of the game is that, no matter how much you improve, there is always room for still more improvement. The learning process is never-ending, and that's one of the reasons that golf is the game of a lifetime. In applying this attitude to the area of tee shots, I think you'll agree that while it's great to know you can hit the ball straight, it's even better if you can "bend" the ball at will when the situation calls for it. This chapter is devoted to showing you how to play two shots—the *power draw* and the *power fade*—that will help you become a truly accomplished driver of the ball.

At this point you might be saying to yourself, "Hey, wait a minute, I'm not a touring pro who can call up a trick shot anytime he wants to. I don't want to get that involved. If I can just learn to hit the driver fairly straight, I will be happy."

Well, if this is your attitude about shotmaking with the driver at the moment, I'd like to encourage you to change it. And here's a little secret that I think will go a long way toward convincing you that you can play the draw and the fade successfully: These two shots are no more difficult to play than the straight tee shot. You do *not* have to perform a series of secret swing manipulations in order to curve the ball left or right off the tee. All you really need is to develop a clear understanding of the laws of geometry that cause the ball to draw or fade, then make the slight adjustments in your setup that allow these laws of geometry to take place. With the proper adjustments, you can then utilize the swing techniques you have just learned, yet still make the ball draw or fade at will.

Developing the power draw and the power fade will help you save strokes over the course of every round you play. These shots will help you cut yardage off certain holes, leaving shorter approach shots. They will also help you to position the ball on the side of the fairway that will leave you with a clear angle to the pin.

In addition, I believe that if you know how to hit both these shots, you are much more likely to consistently drive the ball straight when that's what you want to do. Why? Because the setup for both the draw and the fade provide a sort of frame for your basic setup for the straight drive. That is, you're making setup adjustments that are on either side of the setup for the straight ball. This will always make it simpler for you to get back to your middle ground. The golfer who just vaguely tries to hit the ball straight on every tee shot is much more likely to fall into setup or swing flaws that develop into either a consistent hook or a consistent slice. For the player who develops a slice, for instance, it's much more difficult to get back to the basics of a straight clubhead delivery than it is for the player who knows how to draw and fade the ball. If you're doing a little bit of both all the time, you'll never stray too far off the track.

Let's talk now about the on-course situations in which the draw and the fade will prove valuable. I believe it's very important that you be on the lookout for these various topographical and climatic factors and know when to apply either the draw or the fade to them. You'll find that by analyzing these factors and deciding which way to bend the ball, you'll be getting a much clearer, more specific focus on each and every tee shot, which increases your chances of playing the shot well. And when you get to this point in your shotmaking analysis, you'll truly be playing the game to the hilt and you will be gaining the fullest enjoyment possible.

When to Play the Power Draw

1. *On dogleg left par four holes.* Whenever you're playing a par four whose fairway doglegs sharply to the left, the power draw will help you keep the ball in the fairway and save you valuable yardage. Say the hole in question is 400 yards long and turns left at the 200-yard mark. Say also that when you hit a reasonably solid, straight drive, you get an average of about 230 yards on the shot.

In this situation, your normal straight drive will land in the middle of the fairway. However, because the hole curves left in the landing area, your ball will finish up on the right side of the fairway or even in the right rough. Since the hole's length is measured along the center of the fairway, you're actually making the hole play longer, say 415 yards instead of 400. Thus your 230-yard drive may actually leave you with 185 yards to the center of the green, probably a long iron with a tough angle, to boot.

Meanwhile, with the power draw you can bend the ball around the corner on the fly, with the draw spin upon landing making the ball finish in the left center of the fairway. This should allow you to cut perhaps fifteen yards off the hole, making it play around 385. Also, remember that because of its penetrating flight pattern and additional roll, you'll average about 10 extra yards by playing the power draw. Thus, your second shot will end up being only about 145 yards. That's 40 yards less than you'd have with a straight shot, and you'll enjoy a much better angle to the flag as a bonus.

2. *Holes with a right-to-left fairway contour.* You'll pick up quite a bit of extra yardage if you can start a power draw down the right side of the fairway, so it lands on a right-to-left slope and runs hard to the middle. It's almost like stealing—you can easily get an extra 25 yards of roll, just by putting sidespin that matches the fairway's slope on the ball. NOTE: Play the power draw to a right-to-left fairway only when you have a reasonably open fairway with no major hazards to the left.

3. *Narrow driving holes with a left-to-right fairway contour.* When you're on a tight driving hole in which distance is not crucial and the fairway slopes from left to right, the power draw can help you keep the ball in play. This is because the drawing action of the

ball as it descends will make it "counteract" the left-to-right slope of the fairway, so that it sits down rather quickly rather than running along with the slope. This is a particularly useful shot when the fairway slopes toward woods, water, or out-of-bounds on the right. You'll give up perhaps 10 yards by drawing the ball into the slope, but on holes where keeping it in the fairway is important, this small sacrifice is well worth it.

4. *Into the wind.* You'll always maximize your distance into the wind by utilizing the power draw. Since the shot will be struck with a clubface that's slightly closed in relation to the path of the swing, the ball will shoot out in a lower-than-normal trajectory, so the wind will not affect it as much. The right-to-left draw spin also cuts the wind more effectively than the straight shot. Finally, the power draw will always provide you with a few extra yards of roll after landing.

Depending on the strength of the headwind you're facing, the power draw can easily gain back 20 to 30 yards you would lose with a straight shot.

5. *On long par fours.* The power draw is a great asset if your home course has several longer par fours that you have trouble reaching in regulation. As I mentioned, under normal conditions you'll get about a 10-yard boost with the power draw versus the straight ball. This can be a nice plus, particularly if you are a shorter-than-average hitter. You'll probably reach at least one more green in regulation per round if you know how to hit the power draw on those long fours.

6. *On possibly reachable par fives.* Conversely, say you are a fairly long hitter, one who can drive the ball 240 yards with a solid straight shot. There are probably two par fives on your course that are in the 500-yard range, possibly reachable under the right conditions with your two best shots. With a successful power draw off the tee and also with a fairway wood, you'll pick up about 20 yards on two shots, maybe enough to reach the hole in two shots and pick up a birdie as well.

7. *When playing on hard fairways.* If your course has generally firm, flat fairways, you can pick up ample yardage with the power draw. One word of caution here, however: As when playing the

power draw to a right-to-left sloping fairway, you should have more room in the fairway landing area with the draw, since it's harder to pinpoint the tee shot that gets a long roll.

8. *Driving with a right-to-left wind.* While we'll discuss wind play in detail in Chapter Six, I'd like to point out that you can really gain substantial carry by drawing your tee shots when the wind is blowing from right to left. Whenever you curve the ball in the direction the wind is coming from, the ball will effectively ride the wind so that it carries farther, lands on a shallower than normal trajectory, and gets some extra roll. You can easily pick up 20 to 30 extra yards here with the power draw.

You've now seen eight situations in which simply knowing how to play the power draw can add valuable yards to your tee shots. And you'll gain the yards not by swinging harder or by adding fancy moves to your swing, both of which lead to mishit shots. The beauty of the power draw (as well as the power fade, which we'll discuss later) is that *all the adjustments are made in your setup.* Once you have made these slight setup changes, you can make your normal good swing, yet produce a power draw shot. Let's look at these adjustments now in detail.

Tee High for the Power Draw

Making the ball draw off the tee is simply a matter of slightly altering the delivery of the clubhead from one that produces a perfectly straight shot. For the straight ball, your aim is to deliver the clubhead as it's moving directly along the target line, with the clubface pointing straight to your target. To make the shot draw, you must impart a degree of right-to-left sidespin to the ball. This is accomplished by delivering the clubhead from slightly inside the target line rather than directly along it, with a clubface that's a trifle closed in relation to that swing path.

The first adjustment is to tee the ball higher than you would for a normal drive. If you ordinarily tee up with half the ball above the driver clubface, as is standard, tee it so that nearly the entire ball rests above the clubface.

You might be asking yourself, "How does this help me to hit a draw?" Well, the higher you tee the ball, the more you will swing

When setting up to play a power draw, tee the ball *higher* than normal.

the club around yourself—that is, on a flatter plane—in order to squarely contact a ball resting on a peg about one and a half inches above the ground. Conversely, if the ball were lying on the ground itself, you would naturally make a more vertical, up-and-down swinging motion in order to deliver the club right at ground level at impact.

This flatter swing plane that you get with the higher-teed ball means that your clubhead will naturally enter the impact zone from slightly inside rather than along the target line. Assuming the clubface is pointing straight at the target, this clubhead path means that the club-to-ball contact will impart just a touch of right-to-left spin on the ball. Again, this slight adjustment in your swing path will occur *naturally* when you tee the ball higher than normal. You don't have to consciously decide that you're going to make an extra flat swing when you want to hit the power draw.

Adjust Your Body-to-Clubface Relationship

You may have heard or read in the past that in order to draw your tee shots, you should aim your body and the clubhead well right of the target, then roll your arms and wrists over through impact in

A higher tee promotes a *flatter* swing plane.

order to impart right-to-left spin to the ball. I disagree with this line of thinking because it takes you away from the body-oriented swinging action I advocate, and toward a hands-oriented action. This breeds inconsistency. It's so much easier to adjust the relationship of your hands and your body to the clubface at address, then swing normally, than it is to try to manipulate the clubface closed just the right amount through impact. In fact, it's really impossible to manually close the clubface precisely through the impact zone. Everything happens too fast, so any attempt to close the clubface through impact is just a guessing game. And as we all know, when we guess in golf, we end up wrong more often than right.

So instead, I'd like to teach you to hit the power draw with your

In preparing to hit a *draw* shot, aim the clubface at your target and your body right of target.

setup rather than with independent hand action. You do this by aligning your clubface to the spot you want the ball to finish, then *aligning your body and your grip slightly to the right of this target.*

In setting up to play the power draw shot, aim your clubface exactly where you want the ball to finish. Do *not* align your clubface to the right of where you want the ball to finish. Anytime your clubface is pointing off the line on which you want to finish, it means you will have to manipulate the club through impact to get it back square to the target line. So always set your clubface straight to your ultimate target, whether you're playing a draw, a fade, or a straight shot.

Once you've aimed the clubface correctly, you should *align your entire body slightly right of the target line.* The more you wish to draw the ball, the more you should aim your body to the right. Lines across your feet, knees, hips, and shoulders (your body line) should all align to the same spot to the right of your target line. The larger the draw, the larger the angle should be between your body line and your target line.

Your Grip Matches Your Body Line

An often misunderstood factor in playing the power draw is that you must take an extra-strong grip in order to make the ball go right to left. In one sense, it is true that your grip will be stronger for the power draw than it will be for the straight drive. However, this is so because your hands are merely matching your body alignment, which is a little right of your target. Your hands will be turned a little farther to the right on the club's handle, but as you take your grip, your hands are still in the palms-facing twelve o'clock position relative to your body that they would be in if you were playing a straight shot.

Swing the Club Freely for the Power Draw

Now that you've set up correctly, all you have to do to hit the power draw is execute a swing that feels exactly the same as the one you would use to hit the ball straight, as described in Chapter Two. Start the club away from the ball using the large muscles of your right hip and side; and continue to turn your shoulders while shifting your weight to the inside of your right knee. Then start down by shifting your weight onto the outside of your left foot and turning your left hip and side around in rotary fashion, clearing a path for your arms to swing the club freely through impact.

While the swing feels the same as for a straight shot, the path of your clubhead away from and into the ball will be slightly altered, thanks to your setup adjustments. It is this difference in the clubhead path that will cause the ball to draw.

Because you started out with your body aligned to the right in relation to your clubface and your target line, your normal takeaway path is actually moving the clubhead back more to the inside than it would if you were lined up straight. By the same token, your clubhead path through impact will be straight to your body line, but from the inside in relation to your clubface angle and the target line. Thus, impact imparts a considerable amount of counterclockwise, or draw, spin to the ball as it leaves the clubface. The ball will start out along your body line in a fairly low driving trajectory. It will begin drawing left as it rises to its apex and then falls to the fairway with a little extra roll, finishing along your target line.

It may be hard for you to believe, but that's all you need to know in order to execute the power draw. In reality, this shot is just as easy to hit as the straight ball. It all reverts to the correct body and clubface alignments at address to deliver the clubhead into the ball at the proper angle and with the proper clubface alignment.

Many amateurs to whom I've explained this—particularly those who slice the ball—find it hard to believe that they can play the power draw successfully. It's difficult to do only if your mechanics for the basic straight shot are incorrect. If that is the case, you need to reread the setup and swing fundamentals in Chapters One and Two. If you have these under control, you just have to prove to yourself that this method of playing the power draw really works.

I suggest you build your confidence in the shot first at the practice tee. Pick a range marker or a tree in the distance to represent the line on which you want the ball to finish. Make sure to align the driver clubface straight to this mark. Next, align shoulders, hips, knees, feet, and your grip slightly right of this target. For a 10-yard draw, align yourself 10 yards right; or 20 yards right if you want a 20-yard draw. Once you've done this, my only other advice is to swing the club *freely*. Trust your setup adjustments to make the ball draw and don't try to steer the shot. It will help if you can have a friend monitor your clubface, body, and grip alignments to make sure you are lined up exactly as you intend.

It shouldn't take long before you're getting that solid, rising draw every time you want it on the practice tee. Now you can start using the power draw during actual play. To aid confidence, I suggest you don't force yourself to play the shot on a really demanding driving hole at first. Use it where conditions call for it and where you have a fairly generous fairway to hit to. Once you've hit some successful draw shots and have seen how beneficial the shot can be, you'll find yourself going to it more and more often.

You're well along now toward becoming an accomplished shotmaker with the driver. Let's move on and explore the other side of driver shotmaking: the power fade, and when and how to play it.

When You Need the Power Fade

The power fade is a very useful shot to have in your arsenal, particularly in situations in which accuracy takes precedence over maximum length. You should be aware of the situations where the power fade will help you:

1. *On dogleg right holes.* When you're facing a par four whose fairway bends rather sharply to the right, the power fade is your mirror image of the power draw on dogleg left holes. It will help you keep the ball in the fairway and again cut off some of the hole's yardage.

Let's again assume you're facing a hole that's 400 yards in length, with the fairway bending right roughly at the 200-yard mark. (Make sure that the dogleg is always within reach of your normal tee shot carry. If the hole doglegs late, you should play the shot straight out so you have a clear line to the green on your second shot.) Assuming that your solid straight drive travels some 230 yards, your ball will run beyond this dogleg, finishing on the left side of the fairway or perhaps even running into the left rough. Driving through the dogleg effectively lengthens this hole from 400 yards to about 415, leaving you a difficult 185-yard second shot and likely a tough angle to the green.

The power fade is a great ally here. You can start the ball up the center or right center of the fairway, letting it drift right as it reaches its apex and drops to the fairway, following the hole's curve. The power fade does not actually add distance to your normal drive because, although it will carry about the same distance as normal, it will land softly because of the left-to-right spin imparted. Thus, you can expect about 5 yards less roll with this shot than normal. Still, by cutting the shot 225 yards around the corner, you're effectively making the hole play only about 385 yards, leaving you a more comfortable 160-yard shot from a good angle in the fairway.

2. *On narrow driving holes.* If you're facing a tight fairway, particularly when there's heavy rough on both sides, the power fade is a great shot to have. The reason? It's easier to control than either a draw or a straight ball. This is because the power fade will not roll far after it has landed. If you can land this shape of tee shot in the fairway, it's much more likely to stay there.

Stop to consider the odds of hitting the green from the fairway as opposed to hitting it from a snarled lie in the rough. Even if you're a few yards farther back from the fairway for the shot, the probabilities are always with you when you're hitting it off the short grass. So whenever that fairway looks a little claustrophobic from the tee and the hole's not terribly long, the power fade is a great shot to have.

3. *To fairways that slope sharply right to left.* This situation is similar to the one just listed. Whenever the driving area slopes right to left and there is trouble left such as water or out of bounds, the power fade is a valuable shot to have. Its left-to-right spin as it lands will counteract the ground's slope, and while the fade doesn't run too far anyway, when it lands against a side slope it's almost sure to stay on the short grass if it lands there.

4. *With the wind behind you.* We all play just as many tee shots with the wind behind us as we do into the wind. It only *seems* as though most of them are into the wind.

Whenever the breeze is behind you on the tee, you want to get the ball well up into the air so that the wind carries it for as many extra yards as possible. The power fade will give you maximum distance downwind because it naturally carries a higher trajectory than either a draw or a straight ball. This is because, as we'll see, the clubface is slightly open at impact in relation to the path of the swing; thus it launches the ball with extra loft as well as some left-to-right spin.

If there's a substantial breeze behind you, the added height and air time the power fade offers can add up to 20 extra yards over a tee shot with your normal trajectory.

5. *In wet conditions.* Heavy or rainy conditions cause many amateurs lots of problems. While the fairways and greens are easier to hit because they're softer, the course also plays much longer and it becomes more difficult for the medium or short hitter to reach the greens in regulation. When it's wet, it's best to keep your tee shots in the air as long as possible, and the best way to accomplish this is to hit the power fade.

Actually, the carry you'll get from a well-hit draw, straight tee shot, and fade are all about the same. The reason the left-to-right shot helps here is that if you catch the ball a little thin, as even the best players do sometimes, you'll keep the ball in the air a lot longer and get more distance with the power fade.

6. *Driving with a left-to-right wind.* You can gain an extra 20-plus yards by playing a power fade when there's a good breeze blowing from left to right. The ball's left-to-right spin will allow it to ride the wind for a longer carry. And as with the draw played with a right-to-left wind, the ball will roll farther than normal upon landing. Again, employ this shot when you have a fairly generous landing area, as it's a little harder to pinpoint a tee shot that's riding the wind.

Now that you've seen all the ways a power fade can help you, let's go into the mechanics of playing the shot. As with the power draw, the changes you will make are all in the setup. Once you've made these adjustments, you can hit the power fade with your normal swing. You'll fade the ball by adjusting the path of the clubhead through the impact zone. It's far simpler to modify your setup, then swing normally, than it is to manipulate your swing in an attempt to put left-to-right spin on the ball.

Tee Lower to Encourage Upright Arc

In contrast with the high-teed ball for the drawing tee shot, your first step to playing the power fade is to tee the ball *low*. Tee the ball one-half inch off the ground, so that the top of the ball is barely above the top line of the clubface.

This simple adjustment will make a difference in your swing arc that will promote a left-to-right ball flight. By teeing the ball lower, you will automatically swing in a more upright arc, as opposed to the flatter arc you'll make when the ball is teed high. This more upright arc brings the clubhead into the ball from more directly behind it and on a slightly steeper angle, rather than from inside the target line. The more upright swing path is naturally more conducive to applying left-to-right spin to the ball.

When setting up to play a power fade, tee the ball *lower* than normal.

A lower tee promotes a more *upright* swing plane.

Adjust Your Setup for the Power Fade

The changes you need to make to hit the power fade are basically the opposite of those for the power draw. It's really quite simple. Instead of closing your entire body alignment in relation to your target line, for the power fade you will set your body into a slightly open position. Take note of the word *slightly*. You don't have to make radical changes in your address position to hit a nice power fade or power draw. In either case we're talking about an adjustment of body alignment that's only a few degrees to one side or the other of a straight position.

In setting up to play the power fade, point the clubface at the point at which you want the ball to finish. Don't try to fade the ball by aiming the clubface to the left, then trying to manipulate it open through impact. As with the draw, trying to make the ball move right by using hand action is merely a guessing game. Sometimes you won't open the face enough, other times you'll overdo it and get a wild slice as a result.

Instead, aim the clubface carefully at the target, then align your entire body—shoulders, hips, knees, and feet—slightly to the left of your target.

Make Your Grip Match Your Body Alignment

Once you've correctly aligned the clubface and your body, assume a grip that is neutral or straight in relationship to your body. As you look down, you should see two knuckles on your left hand, the same as you would for a straight shot or a draw. However, because your body alignment is slightly open and your hands are neutral in relation to your body, this also means that your hands will be turned fractionally to the left on the club handle from where they would be for a straight shot.

You're now prepared to hit a solid power fade while taking your normal swing. Try to make exactly the same swing movements outlined in Chapter Two. Draw the club away from the ball and turn your right hip, making a nice weight transfer onto your right side; then start down by planting your weight on the outside of your left

In preparing to hit a *fade* shot, aim the clubface at your target and your body left of target.

foot, and turn your left hip around to the rear to generate force and to make room for your arms to swing through the impact zone. You do *not* need to make any independent moves with your hands and wrists to produce the power fade.

The only other swing advice I want to emphasize here is that you should make sure to retain that flexed-back right wrist that is key to all basic shotmaking. Not only will it help you hold your power through the impact zone, but it's of particular importance when playing the power fade. Any "flippiness" of the hands and wrists that shuts the clubface through impact could result in a big pull hook instead of a shot that starts a little left, then drifts right.

You'll enjoy developing the power fade on the practice tee. As with the power draw, pick out a target where you want the ball to finish and align your clubface precisely at that spot. Then align your entire body (and your grip) to a second marker just left of your target line. Again, it will help to have a friend verify your correct alignment. Strive to make a sound, no-nonsense swing that delivers the clubhead through the ball along the line of your body. Trust the shot to fade rather than trying to make it fade. It will!

Once you have confidence and command of the power fade on the practice tee, you can put it to use on those dogleg right or tighter holes on your home course. It's a great feeling to know you can be a shotmaker with the driver. More important, you'll find yourself saving yardage and putting yourself in position for better approach shots to the pin.

Let's wrap up this chapter with a review of the key factors for playing the draw and the fade.

**RITSON'S
REVIEW**

The Power Draw
- Be aware of the types of holes and shotmaking conditions that encourage the power draw.
- Tee the ball up higher than normal.
- Align your driver clubface to the spot you want the ball to finish.
- Align your body and your grip to a point slightly right of your ultimate target.
- Make your normal, free swing along the path set up by your body line.

The Power Fade
- Know the circumstances in which a soft left-to-right flight off the tee will benefit you.
- Tee the ball lower to promote a more upright swing plane.
- Align your clubface to where the shot should finish.
- Carefully align yourself to a secondary point that's slightly left of your target.
- Swing normally along your body line and keep your right wrist flexed back through impact.

4

SHORT GAME WIZARDRY

How to pitch, chip, and putt like a pro

If you are an occasional weekend player who shoots around 100, if you're a 90 shooter, or even if you're a low handicapper, you'll definitely benefit from gaining some magic in your short game. By providing you with wedge magic on full shots, half shots, greenside flips, and the pitch-and-run, along with improved techniques for your chipping and putting, this chapter can make a remarkable difference in the scores you shoot.

Most golfers don't realize it, but if you add up all your full and partial wedge shots, all your greenside chips, and all your putts, these account for more than 50 percent of all the strokes you play. Since pitching, chipping, and putting make up more than half the game of golf, it makes sense that sharpening your techniques in these areas is the surest way to lower scores.

Anyone can learn to be a short game magician. By *short game* I'm referring to all shots ranging from a full pitching wedge or full sand wedge all the way down to the short putts. You do not have to be a great athlete to hit a 50- or 100-yard wedge stiff to the pin, or to sink a 15-foot putt. Conversely, I will admit that it takes more athletic skill than most amateurs possess to blast tee shots 250 to

275 yards, while keeping them consistently in the fairway. Certainly, you can and will improve your tee shots and other shots with the long clubs by following the principles in Chapters One through Three. But there are physical limits to how much you will improve, which vary from player to player. Anytime you take less than a full swing, however, there are no physical limits to how well you can play the stroke. By learning the short game methods in this chapter and dedicating the bulk of your practice time to making these shots second nature, there is no reason you can't become a great short game player. I don't care if you're a man or a woman, a youngster or a senior citizen; mastering the short game is the key to knocking a sizable number of strokes off your score.

Now that I've convinced you, I hope, how important the short game is, let's move to a position about 100 yards from the hole— the outer limit of the short game.

The Full Pitch Shot

A 100-yard pitch shot will normally represent a full or close to full pitching wedge shot for most male amateurs. Stronger players may be able to cover this distance with a full sand wedge. In either case, the shotmaking principles are the same. For the ladies, 100 yards might be a little outside wedge range; if this is the case, apply this advice to your normal range for the pitching wedge, which may be 70 to 90 yards out.

After you've assessed the shot and are ready to step up to the ball, assume your standard grip. Your left thumb should rest at the one o'clock position on the handle with two knuckles visible on that hand. It's a good idea to choke down on the club about 1 inch more than normal, so that at least 2 inches of the grip are visible below your left little finger.

Assume a stance that is a little narrower than the width of your shoulders. As almost always, the ball should be positioned opposite the inside of your left heel. Also, pull your left foot back an inch or two from the target line, into a slightly open position. This will help you visualize your target better.

Your hips should be canted toward the target, with your head

In setting up to play
the full pitch shot, *cant*
your hips toward the
target.

slightly behind the ball and your right shoulder a bit lower than your left. As was stated in Chapter One, for the wedge you should place 70 percent of your weight on your left foot, which encourages a crisp downward blow through the ball.

As you settle in to play the shot, make sure to feather the club lightly behind the ball; never push the sole of the club down hard against the turf or else you will tend to catch the club in the grass on the takeaway, and perhaps even move the ball and incur a penalty. Stay in motion just before you start the swing, as this will also aid in making a smooth, rhythmic takeaway.

I describe the takeaway for the full wedge pitch as a pulling-back action of the entire right side. Your right hip, right shoulder, and right arm should all make a generous turn toward the right rear. Make no conscious manipulations of your hands or wrists. As your hands reach about hip height, your wrists will gradually begin to hinge, but this is only in response to the weight of the clubhead. Swing the club up to a compact three-quarter position, with the clubshaft about halfway between perpendicular and parallel.

On the downswing, it will be the large muscles of the *left* side that lead the action—your left hip, shoulder, and upper arm. Start the downswing by rolling your weight onto the outside of your left foot, then rotate your left hip around to your left rear. Once you've rotated the left hip, pull down strongly with the left shoulder and upper arm while keeping the hands inactive. As on the backswing, your arms and hands must follow the movement rather than lead it. I disagree strongly with those who instruct that you should keep your body still on wedge shots and let the arms and hands dominate the action. You will never be as consistent if you're relying on your smaller muscles instead of your larger ones.

The only thought you should have regarding your hands on the downswing is to *delay* the release of your right wrist cock as long as possible. This is the key to imparting maximum spin to the ball. As your arms and hands approach the hitting zone, think of maintaining the pressure in your right knee and pulling the butt of the club down, while never allowing your right hand to pass your left until well after the ball has left the clubface. I believe the most damaging fault of the average player with the wedge is that he tries to lift the ball into the air with a scooping action of the right hand. Usually this results in the deflating flubbed or "fat" shot that flies barely half the intended distance. Conversely, scooping with the right hand can also cause you to hit a very low powerful shot that races over the green.

When playing the full pitch, let the left hip, shoulder, and upper arm *lead* the downswing action.

There's no need to try to lift the ball. Let the high-lofted pitching and sand wedges work for you. Pull the club down with your left hand while you make no conscious effort with your right hand. The descending blow that results produces maximum acceleration and forces the ball to climb up the clubface at impact, creating maximum spin.

Here's a drill to help you ingrain the feeling of holding that right hand back through the impact zone. I call it the "dagger drill." Position yourself as if you are halfway into your downswing, with your wrists still fully cocked so that the butt end of the grip is pointing down at the ball. Now move your right hand onto the metal shaft a few inches below the grip. While holding the shaft back with your right hand, try to pull the butt of the club straight down at the ball. You'll feel the resistance along the outside of your left arm and shoulder. This is the sensation you want to develop in your actual swing. Pull the club down with that left arm leading and keep that right wrist cocked until as late as possible. You should have the sensation that your right hand is chasing your left through the impact zone, with both wrists maintaining the angles that were first established at address.

I can't emphasize strongly enough that the key to crisp, controlled wedge play is to keep the right hand from taking over. If anyone ever suggests that you play these shots with your right hand dominating the shot and rolling over your left through impact, politely ignore the advice.

If you've executed the wedge downswing properly, you'll finish with your weight on your left foot, with your body facing directly at the target in a relaxed upright position. As for the ball flight, assuming the lie is good, the ball will actually take off a shade lower than it would with your old scooping action. This is to be expected and is in fact very desirable. Because of the heavy backspin imparted, the ball will rise quickly to its apex, and drop to the green at a steep angle and with plenty of spin. Depending on the firmness of the greens and assuming you've played the shot from a good lie, the ball will take one or two soft bounces before biting in and coming to a rest. One final piece of advice: Once you've mastered this wedge technique, you can become a little bolder with these shots. As long as you're playing to well-conditioned greens, don't hesitate to fly the ball all the way to the hole.

The Half Wedge Shot

You know, I watch golf tournaments on television nearly every weekend, just like every dedicated fan does. And there's a certain commentary on a shotmaking situation that never ceases to amaze me. This occurs when a tour star is playing a par five hole that he can't reach in two shots. So often I hear the announcer say something to this effect: "He won't quite be able to get it home, so instead of hitting a wood to within forty or fifty yards of the hole, he'll lay up with an iron. This way he'll leave himself with a full wedge so he can really put some spin on the ball."

This approach to such a situation really baffles me. Because I *know* that you, I, or any tour pro can put plenty of "stop" on the ball with the half wedge shot played from 40 to 60 yards out. This being the case, I think it's really harmful advice to suggest that it's smart golf to leave the ball 100 yards or more from the hole when you have the opportunity to put it within half that distance. I don't care what anyone says: Assuming that you can keep the ball in the fairway so the lie is good, the shorter the shot you have, the closer you should be able to hit the ball to the hole. Yes, I've heard all that logic about how much easier it is to hit the ball closer to the hole with a full swing as opposed to a half shot, because it's easier to judge a full swing and how far the shot is going to travel. My feeling is that this reasoning is erroneous. If you took it to its extreme, it would suggest that you could be as accurate with a driver swing as you can with the shortest swing of all, a putting stroke. It just doesn't add up.

Look at it this way: If you're 100 yards out and execute the shot with a combined 5 percent error in distance and direction (a fairly good shot), this means the ball will finish 5 yards, or 15 feet, from the cup. If you make a 5 percent error from 50 yards out, your ball will stop only 2½ yards, or 7 to 8 feet, from the hole. Knowing as I do that I can put enough spin on the ball with the half wedge from the fairway to make it stick near virtually any pin placement, given the choice I'll go for the half wedge every time. Now, let me show you how to make the spinning half wedge part of your shotmaking arsenal.

The first point is to play the half wedge shot with a sand wedge if the lie is reasonably good. The sand wedge offers approximately 55 degrees of loft as opposed to an average of 50 degrees with a standard pitching wedge. This 5-degree difference in loft is actually more than the differences in loft between the numbered irons, which average between 3 and 4 degrees of loft difference per club. So take advantage of the substantially added height and backspin the sand wedge offers whenever you have the opportunity. The only time you should go with the pitching wedge is when the lie is very tight, as on hardpan, when there's more chance that the larger flange of the sand wedge may bounce off the hard surface and cause a mishit.

The setup should be similar to that for the full pitch, with just a few simple adjustments. Assume your standard grip, again choking down on the club an extra inch. Your stance should be just an inch or two narrower than for the full wedge pitch. Your left arm and the clubshaft should form a straight line down to the ball, which keeps your hands slightly ahead. Keep your head behind the ball with your right shoulder lower than your left. This setup should make you feel as though you're preparing to make an underhanded toss toward the target.

Two small adjustments from your full wedge setup are as follows:

1. Open your stance a little more than normal and also open the clubface in relation to the target line. When you swing, these adjustments will automatically help you to cut across the ball, creating a spin that gives the shot more stopping power than perfectly straight contact will.

2. Distribute your weight 50/50 for the half wedge instead of keeping most of it on your left foot. This will help you play a more sweeping shot with only a slight divot. This more sweeping action will also help give the half shot more immediate height and stopping power, as opposed to the more downward blow for the full wedge.

Once you've settled over the shot, take the club back slowly and in a fairly low, wide arc. I do *not* recommend a quick pickup with the hand on the half wedge shot. Again, feel like the backswing movement is initiated with your right hip and right shoulder, while your hands merely go along for the ride. The wrists will hinge just a trifle of their own accord as you start the backswing.

Experience will teach you the proper length of backswing for the shot at hand. Granted, this is the "disadvantage" the full-swing proponents point to in playing a half wedge shot. However, to me it's a disadvantage in theory rather than in reality. Consider it this way: Say you try to lay up so you have a "perfect" full-length wedge shot. This means you should leave yourself 90 yards away for a full sand wedge or, alternatively, 100 yards for a full pitching wedge. I ask you, how often will your layup leave you with exactly 90 or 100 yards to the flag? More than likely you'll have 82 yards or 97 yards or 106 yards. Do you see my point? If you were so talented that you could leave the ball a precise number of yards from the hole, you would be the greatest player alive and you wouldn't be reading this book.

Every wedge shot requires some degree of feel. If you are careful in assessing the shot, developing a nice clear picture of it in your mind as you step up to it, your instincts will help you judge the proper length of backswing needed. Of course, practice in this area will definitely improve your play even more. As you work on your half wedge techniques on the practice tee, always pick out a marker of some sort where you want the ball to finish. It won't take long before you can adjust the wedge swing confidently for any yardage.

Within the framework I've just described, I recommend that you make a relatively compact backswing for the length of shot at hand. One thing you want to avoid is an overly long, loose arm swing which requires you to decelerate on the downswing. If you are 50 yards from the hole, chances are you'll need only take the club back to where the shaft is perpendicular to the ground or just a touch beyond. Just make sure to lead the backswing with the large muscles of your right hip area—never swing the arms so that they outrun the turn of the body.

You'll start the club down in the same fashion as with the longer

The half wedge shot calls for a very *short* backswing, particularly from around 50 yards out from the green.

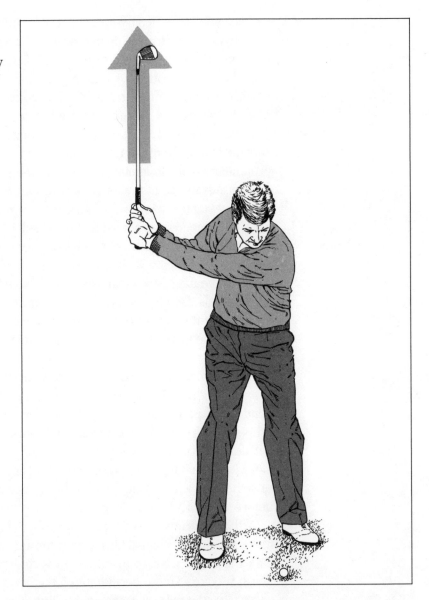

shots, with your weight shifting to your left foot while your left hip accelerates toward the left rear. You should *never* accelerate the club with your hands and arms on the downswing, no matter how short the pitch. The secret to hitting a crisp, quick-stopping short wedge is to keep your right wrist flexed back through and beyond

In hitting the half
wedge, a critical
technical priority is to
brush your chin with
your right shoulder on
the downswing.

impact. After your hips have made the initial move downward,
simply pull the club through with your upper left arm. The right
wrist should remain flexed backward, leaving the clubhead lagging
behind also. To promote a sweeping action of club through ball,
brush your chin with your right shoulder.

If you play the shot in the manner described, the face of your sand wedge will accelerate into the ball at impact. The ball will grip the clubface before leaving it, and since you've cut across the shot slightly with an open clubface, it will also pick up some left-to-right cut spin. The result is a shot that will fly high and drop to the green very softly, taking one soft bounce to the right. Again, be aggressive in planning the shot and try to fly the ball almost all the way to the cup.

Now, with just a little practice, you should be ready to stick the ball close with the wedge from any distance. So let's move close to the green and go to work perfecting your shotmaking there.

The Greenside Flip Shot

On many well-maintained courses that are not too heavily bunkered around the greens, you'll likely find yourself in medium to heavy greenside rough at least a couple of times per round. If the pin is located on the near side so there's not much green to work with, and/or the green is firm and fast, you may have your work cut out for you to save par. Before we get into the technique for the greenside flip, though, let's have a word about the mental outlook which will lead to handling the shot successfully.

I notice that from greenside rough, many middle and high handicappers create completely different, rather exotic moves in some vague attempt to play the "perfect" shot. The typical club-level golfer plays the ball in front of his left foot with his hands behind the ball at address and with a very laid-back clubface. Then he tries to make nearly a full swing while slicing the clubface under the ball in an attempt to pop it almost straight up. This may work occasionally. More often, however, he'll hit the shot only a couple of feet, so that he must play practically the same shot all over again. Instead of saving par, he scores double bogey—or worse.

I believe in playing the shot with a much sounder, basic technique that will quite often allow you to save your par, while ensuring that you *always* put the ball on the green. From fair to good lies, you will be able to stop the ball close to the hole or perhaps even hole the shot! There will be occasions where the ball is really sitting down in heavy rough, where you may have to accept having the ball run

In setting up to play the greenside *flip* shot, be sure to "open" your stance, by pointing your feet left of target.

several feet past the hole. However, I have no doubt that if you follow this advice, you'll increase your "ups and downs" and cut back on missed shots from these ticklish situations.

Let's assume your ball is 50 feet from the hole. You have 30 feet of rough and fringe with possibly some upslope to carry, then 20 feet of green to work with.

Your setup should be very similar to that for the half wedge shot. Always use your sand wedge, gripping down on the handle a bit.

Both your stance and the clubface should be slightly open and the ball opposite your left heel. Position your weight evenly between the feet and hover the club lightly on the grass to prevent it from sagging on the backswing.

This is really the one position in which it is okay to pick up the club a little more abruptly, by cocking your wrists slightly as you start back. Continue up until your hands are at about hip height for a shot of this distance, so the clubshaft is not quite to perpendicular. NOTE: You need to practice in these situations to develop an accurate feel for the length of backswing and total force you'll need for each individual position. If the grass is extra deep, or wet, or lying with the blades against you, you must make a much fuller backswing than in situations in which the grass is not too deep and/or it is running with you.

Once you've reached the top of this slightly more wristy backswing, start down by rotating your left hip around to the left and letting your arms and hands follow. Once you've cleared the hip, pull down and through with the left arm leading. Do not let your right wrist uncock, even in the follow-through. You should finish with the clubface pointing toward the sky.

At impact, the ball will roll up the slightly opened clubface so that it pops high out of the rough and lands softly. Unlike with pitch shots played from the fairway, some grass will slip between the clubface and ball at impact. This reduces the amount of backspin on the shot, so allow for a little roll. In this example, where you have 20 feet of green to work with on a medium-speed green, try to land the ball 8 to 10 feet onto the green and let it roll the remaining distance.

You will encounter a situation occasionally where the ball is nestled down severely in the greenside rough. This makes it very difficult to get the flange of your sand wedge under the ball so that it pops out high and softly. In these cases, I recommend you play the shot in the same manner except that you square up the leading edge of your sand wedge, keeping your hands slightly ahead of the ball. Use the swing force you judge necessary to get through the thick grass, again aiming to fly the ball 8 to 10 feet onto the green. I feel this slight margin for error is worthwhile.

When playing the flip shot, you'll usually only have to swing your hands up to about *hip height*.

If the ball comes out of the deep rough as planned, it will fly a little lower and run a bit more because of the straight clubface position at address. The result will usually be that the ball finishes 10 to 20 feet past the flag, still within makeable range. It's a small price to pay for safety in these sticky situations.

Next time you're at the pitching green, create different lengths of shot, different lies, different angles, and different amounts of

In hitting the flip shot, concentrate on trying to point the clubface toward the *sky* in the follow-through.

green to work with. Marry the technique described with the feel you need for the various shots and you'll find your short pitches saving you strokes in short order.

The Pitch-and-Run

You don't always have to hit a high, biting shot from pitching or sand wedge distance. In fact, there are a number of situations in which the low, running shot from around 100 yards or less is the smartest play. Let's first take a look at these situations that call for the pitch-and-run:

1. *When the pin is at the back of a deep green.* Let's say you're 90 yards away from the flag, which is set 30 yards back from the front edge of a green that is 35 yards deep. You have a clear line to the pin. In cases like this, it doesn't make sense to try to fly the ball all the way to the hole and make it stop dead. If you carry it a bit too far or the ball hits a hard spot, you're over the green with little space to work with. It's also very common to back off on your original thought of flying the ball to the hole, so you come up way short. A lower running shot here will usually help you get it closer.

2. *When the pin is back and the terrain behind the green is treacherous.* Quite a few courses feature elevated greens with steep embankments over the back. Flying the green on such holes virtually guarantees a bogey. When the flag is on the back half of such a green and the front is open, play the percentages and use the pitch-and-run.

3. *With the pin on the upper tier of a two-level green.* You'll run into shots of 100 yards or less where the pin is placed just over a crest in the green, so that only an absolutely perfect shot will carry the crest and stop dead by the hole. The high pitch can be extra sticky here, however, because often the top tier of a two-level green is drier and firmer than the rest of the green, thus it's even harder to stop the ball quickly. Using the front half of the green and running the ball over the crest makes better sense.

4. *In windy conditions with the front of the green open.* The high wedge is always tougher to judge and execute in a strong breeze, no matter what its direction. If there are no bunkers, mounds, or other hazards to carry, take advantage by playing a lower shot that is easier to control.

Let's talk for a minute about club selection for pitch-and-run shots. You needn't always play these with a wedge; in fact, you should never use the sand wedge if you want the ball to run. And there will be situations in which you'll find that a 9-, 8-, or even a 7-iron will provide the optimum carry and roll for the shot at hand. For example, say you're only 50 yards from the hole with 25 yards of green before the cup. You may only wish to carry the ball 30 yards and run it the remaining 20 to the hole. An 8- or 9-iron is likely your best bet here. Or suppose you're playing a 90-yard pitch-and-run into a strong wind, and again you have plenty of green. Here, since you want to keep the ball down even more than normal, a pitch-and-run with the 7-iron might be the wisest selection. Don't be afraid to use your creativity and explore all the angles when you're in a pitch-and-run situation.

The pitch-and-run is one area of short game play in which I do not emphasize keeping the wrists straight through impact. The technique I'm about to explain, along with the selection of a bit less loft to begin with, will provide you with a lower trajectory and a shot that releases instead of stopping dead after one bounce.

The address position for the pitch-and-run is basically the same from all distances. The only difference will be in the width of your stance. From 100 yards out, your stance will be just slightly narrower than shoulder width, while from 50 yards your heels should be just 6 inches or so apart. Other than that, everything else is the same regardless of distance. Grip the club normally, choking down an extra inch or so, and set at least 70 percent of your weight on your left side. Position the ball opposite the center of your stance with your hands a good 2 inches in front of the ball, to encourage a crisp downward hit.

In executing the swing for the pitch-and-run, you will be adding a bit of hand action to the body-dominated backswing and downswing that I've explained for the lofted pitches. While I still encourage you to pull the club back with your right hip and right shoulder and to swing down with your left hip moving in rotary fashion, you must also use your hands to some degree. As you draw the club back with your right hip, *fan* the clubface open slightly by turning your hands just a little in a clockwise direction. Then, as your left side pulls the club down into the impact zone, roll your hands a touch in counterclockwise fashion so that through impact, the toe of the club is passing the heel. This closing action through impact will make the ball jump off the clubface rather than roll up the clubface as on the lofted pitch.

Past impact, finish low with the hands chasing the clubhead, so that you're pointing the clubhead at the target.

An important address priority, in setting up to play the pitch-and-run, is to set the hands *ahead* of the ball.

Go out to your course some evening and play to a green and pin position that calls for a pitch-and-run shot. Play some running pitch shots from 50 yards, 75 yards, and 100 yards. Use your pitching wedge or, if you think the shot calls for it, a less lofted iron. Gradually you'll develop your instincts for the length of swing required and also the carry and roll you get with each swing and with the various clubs. As you develop confidence in your ability to

It's critical that you "fan" the clubface open on the backswing, when playing the pitch-and-run.

hit the ball close, start working the pitch-and-run shot into your regular rounds. It will prove a valuable addition to your short game repertoire.

Greenside Chipping Techniques

Let's talk now about your approach to the basic chipping game. I'm referring to those situations that come up several times per round where you've hit a reasonable approach shot that's bounced no more than 6 to 8 feet off the green and is lying on the manicured fringe grass rather than in deep rough. Depending on pin placement, your ball may be anywhere between 20 and 60 feet from the cup.

In the many rounds I play with middle- to high-handicap amateurs, it's surprising how many of them seem to overlook what a great opportunity this basic chip shot presents. So often, the amateur plays the shot quickly, leaving it 10 feet long or short of the cup. It's as if he's assumed that since he missed the green, even if only by a tiny bit, he should more or less settle for bogey. After all, he seems to reason, he averages a bogey or more per hole anyway, so a chip and two putts for bogey won't really hurt his score.

I can't tell you how much I disagree with this line of thinking. This is a position in which the quality of your mental approach to the shot, when multiplied several times per round and hundreds of times over a season of play, will really have an effect on the scores you shoot. When you miss the green, you must carefully gather yourself to play a good shot. Sure, there will be times when your position is such that you have to be a little conservative and settle for bogey. But when you're just off the green preparing to play the basic chip, you must always think in terms of getting the ball up and down in two. And you should also recognize the opportunity to hole out certain chip shots and play aggressively.

The tour pro's attitude is completely different from most amateurs when it comes to the standard chip shot. If you've watched really great chippers like Ray Floyd and Seve Ballesteros over the years, you know these players are never thinking bogey if they've just missed the green. When they're within 40 feet of the hole and there are no extreme undulations along the line of chip, these players are thinking of holing the shot. On longer or more severely undulating chips, they focus on what's needed to get the ball within easy one-putt range, but in either case they are very intent on obtaining a very positive result. Nine times out of ten they do.

Now, let's think about the basic chip shot for a moment. As we'll see, it's a very uncomplicated shot. There is nothing that Floyd or Ballesteros can do from this position that you can't do. The only difference is that they actively try to hold these shots, and they have years and years of practice and positive experience in doing so. Yes, you'll need lots of practice to become a truly great chipper, but developing a highly positive mental approach is a critical first step to becoming proficient around the green.

I teach my students to use one basic chipping stroke and vary the club they select depending on the amount of carry and roll required. This is a much simpler method than using one favorite club extensively, then trying to adjust your stroke for each situation. There may be a regular in your weekend foursome who seems to get fair results chipping with the same club, but believe me, this makes matters much more complicated than they need to be. Use all the tools that are available to you.

On chip shots, be sure to keep your head *down* an extra split second in the hitting area.

On every chip, you want to make the shot react as much like a putt as possible. That is, you want to loft the ball just a couple of feet onto the putting surface, then let it run the rest of the way to the hole. If you're just a few feet off the green but 60 feet from the hole, you might want to use a 6-iron. For a 25-foot chip with 15 feet of green to work with, you should go with a sand wedge. There are all types of situations between these two that may call for a 7-, 8-, or 9-iron, or a pitching wedge chip. Bear in mind that your club selection will also depend to a great degree on whether the shot is uphill or downhill, and whether the green is slow or fast.

Your stance for the chip should be narrow, with the heels four to six inches apart and open, which helps you visualize your target. On all chips you want to make sure you contact the ball first with a descending blow. For this reason, play the ball a bit back in your stance, opposite your left thigh. Keep most of your weight on your left side at address and throughout the stroke.

The stroke itself should be relatively compact, with the clubhead staying low to the ground on the backswing and downswing. Since the chip is such a short shot, simply control the club's movement with your hands and arms while keeping your wrists firm through-out the stroke.

On the downswing, always make sure your left hand pulls down and leads the clubface through impact. Keep your head steady throughout the stroke and wait an extra second before looking up— insurance against peeking and hitting the shot heavy.

Practice this simple, yet effective method while making sure to use the right club, and you'll find yourself chipping the ball "stiff" a high percentage of the time. And when the situation is right, don't be afraid to think "sink."

Putting Technique

We're now on the putting green, where most matches are won or lost at every level of play. Whether you're a scratch player or shoot around 100, you'll take an average of 40 percent of your strokes on the green. Surely that's incentive enough to make you want to improve in this, the most frustrating area of the game of golf. Improved putting is your surest route to lower scores.

There are sundry styles of putting strokes, and the number of methods seems to be expanding, with cross-handed styles and the many variations on the long-putter theme. While I don't want to criticize anything that works, I believe that many of the unconventional methods you see contribute more to the player's confidence than to providing any tangible physical advantage. I really don't think there's anything that can beat a solid, repeating stroke pattern utilizing a conventional-length putter and a regular (as opposed to cross-handed) putting grip.

Before going into the mechanics, though, let's discuss the mental aspects of preparing to sink a putt. Do you realize that many putts are made or missed long before you've even hit them? If you don't start by making the correct read of the slope in the green, then lining the putter up perfectly to match that read, your chances of holing putts consistently are slim. You should begin *reading* a putt even as you approach the green, not just when you are squatting down behind the ball. Take note of the lay of the land surrounding the green if your course is built on hilly terrain. Does the ground surrounding the green slope in any particular direction? If so, the green may slope in that direction a little more than it might appear to when you are actually standing on the green.

Likewise, take note of any grain in the green, meaning the direction toward which the grass tends to lie. If there is a noticeable grain in the green's surface, the ball will tend to drift in that direction as it loses its speed. Grain is more prevalent on the Bermuda grass greens of the south and southwest, while softer-bladed bentgrass greens, prevalent in the cooler climates, will show little grain effect. However, keep in mind that all strains of grass will also grow toward any bodies of water located near the green. Whether it's the natural grain of the grass or the fact that a body of water is nearby, this is a factor to include in your read of the green.

Of course, correctly assessing the slope of the green along your line of putt is the key element to a good read. However, in addition to the slope itself, the ball will react differently if the putt has been stroked firmly (less break) or lightly (more break). Keep in mind also that, given the same amount of slope, a putt will break much more sharply on a fast surface than on a slower one, where the longer grass blades slow the ball's sideways as well as forward movement. In general, though, I believe most amateurs tend to underestimate the amount of break in any given putt. Therefore, the majority of their misses will finish below the hole, on the low side. So I recommend that, if anything, you allow for a touch more break than you might have been considering. As long as the ball is above the hole and working its way down the slope, it still has a chance to drop. Once the ball has gone below the hole, it has no chance.

Let's talk more about the setup and mechanics of a great stroke. I recommend a reverse overlap grip, in which the left forefinger overlaps the last three fingers of the right hand. The benefit of such a unique hold, common to most top pros, is that all of your right-hand fingers are on the grip, which helps promote better feel and will assist the stroking motion I'd like you to use.

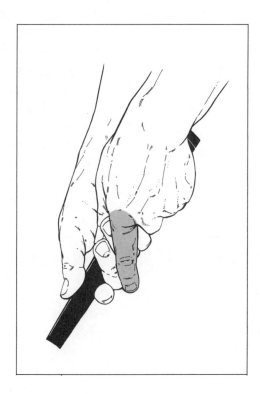

Employing a *reverse overlap* grip will enhance your feel on putts.

While we're on the subject of the grip, I suggest that whatever style of putter you choose, you use a putter with a relatively thick handle. The thicker grip will help you make the one-piece, firm-wristed stroking motion we'll talk about shortly.

Once you've determined the line of putt and judged how hard to stroke it, you're ready to step up to the ball. As you're doing this, it's very important to focus on the starting line of your putt and to align your putterblade precisely with this starting line. Suppose you have a putt that breaks 18 inches to the right. Focus on a spot just a foot or so in front of the ball on a line that would end up 18 inches left of the hole, if the ball were to roll straight. Align the blade with this spot and try to stroke the ball right over it at the proper speed. There's a tremendous temptation to align the blade correctly, then instinctively make your stroke almost directly at the hole itself. The result is that the ball starts below your intended starting line and winds up missing the hole on the low side, in this case to the right. So stick with your spot and forget about the hole on breaking putts.

I believe in a straight address position with your body aligned with the starting line of the putt. However, many good putters prefer a slightly open address position, as it helps them see the line better. This is acceptable, too. The ball should be positioned opposite your left heel, the lowest point in the stroke, with your hands a bit ahead of the ball.

As you address the ball prior to the stroke and during the stroke itself, keep a relatively light grip pressure and sole the club very lightly behind the ball. Incidentally, I think it's a good idea to keep the clubface a fraction of an inch behind the ball itself—insurance that you don't inadvertently move it and incur a penalty stroke. Furthermore, setting the putterblade behind the ball will promote a low-back stroke.

You can simplify your putting action tremendously by, in effect, executing the stroke with one hand only. Right-handed players should supply the energy for the stroke with their right hand, arm, and shoulder (while the left hand simply goes along for the ride).

Try to make a very firm-wristed stroke. Your right hand and arm

Set the putterblade down "behind" the ball, to promote a smooth low-back stroke and prevent a penalty stroke.

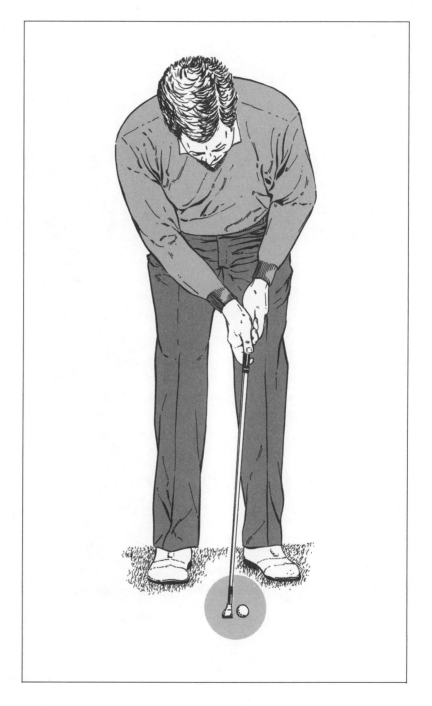

Accelerating the putter through the ball is very important to good scoring on the greens.

should pull the handle back and push it through in a one-piece, pistonlike movement. Probably the best example of a proponent of this kind of stroking action is Jack Nicklaus. Mind you, I'm not asking you to use this stroking action because Jack Nicklaus does, but rather because it's a highly effective, simple, repeatable method.

As you execute the stroke, make sure you keep your right wrist in that locked-back position, which is a key to so many different shots. Never allow that right wrist to flip the clubface forward, which produces erratic contact and clubface alignment on a putt, just as it can for a full shot.

Your stroke should feel rhythmic, with perhaps even a tiny pause at the top of the backstroke. However, you should always feel you are accelerating the club handle (and with it the clubface) through the ball. Quitting at impact is an extremely common putting problem, even for the best tour pros. There's a terrific temptation to watch the ball as it leaves the putterface, since you're anxious to see if you're going to hole it. What happens very often is you actually begin to lift your head as the clubface is contacting the ball. The result is that you come out of the putt in exactly the same way you might come off the ball on a full shot. And, just as that full shot finishes short and right of the hole (for right-handers), whenever you come out of a putt, it's going to leak to the right and probably come up short, too. So discipline yourself to *accelerate* your stroke through the ball and keep your head rock steady. On putts of less than ten feet, the best advice is that you not look up at all—just listen as the ball rattles the cup. It will do so a lot more often if you keep your head in a steady position and accelerate the handle through the ball.

Let's review everything we've covered in this chapter. If you retain a clear image of these principles as you practice them, your short game will begin to work magic in a very short time.

RITSON'S REVIEW

The Full Wedge Pitch
- Keep the stance relatively wide, with your weight toward the left side.
- Use the large muscles of the hips to lead your backswing and downswing turns.
- Pull down with the left arm while keeping the hands "quiet."
- Finish with your entire body facing the target.
- Make a one-piece follow-through.

The Half Wedge Shot
- Play the ball opposite your left heel, with a slightly opened clubface.
- Distribute your weight equally on both feet.
- Take the club back to a perpendicular position or just beyond for the 50-yard shot.
- Accelerate the left hip to power the downswing.
- Keep the right wrist flexed back through impact.
- Make a one-piece follow-through.

The Greenside Flip
- Open both your stance and the clubface of a sand wedge.
- Use a slight wrist cock on the backswing.
- Pull the club down with your left hand.
- Follow through with the clubface pointing toward the sky.

The Pitch-and-Run
- Address the ball in the center of a square stance, with your head directly over the ball and most of your weight on the left side.
- Fan the club slightly open on the backswing, then make the toe pass the heel through impact.
- Finish with the clubface pointing at the target.

Greenside Chipping
- Pick the club that will land the ball on the green and run it to the hole.

- Narrow the stance and keep more weight on your left side.
- Position the ball opposite your right heel.
- Use an arm swing, while keeping the wrists firm.

Putting Technique
- In assessing the line, check the lie of the land around the green.
- Set up carefully along the target line on breaking putts.
- Set up with your eyes over the target line.
- Let the right hand and arm dominate the stroke while keeping the wrists firm.
- Accelerate through the ball.
- Listen, don't look, for the ball to drop.

5 SAND SAVES

Here are some proven tips on how to perform magic in sand traps

If you've ever watched the pros play in person or seen them compete on television, you're probably envious of their shotmaking prowess from sand. Out of the bunker, the tour pros are just phenomenal. If any of them faces an average greenside bunker shot, one that poses no exceptional problems of stance or lie, chances are he'll hit the ball within easy one-putt range almost every time—or even knock it in the hole! In fact, it has reached the point that if a tour player happens to hit a sand shot, say, 15 feet past the hole, the TV analysts nearly fall out of their chairs in amazement at how "bad" a shot the player has hit.

The tour pros are so adept at getting up and down in two from sand that they'll often *aim* for bunkers. If one can't quite carry a bunker to reach a long par five in two, he'll try to hit into the bunker rather than lay up, figuring the odds are better of getting up and down from the sand. Or, if he's driven into deep rough on a par four and knows his approach won't hold the green, he'll try to put his next shot in a bunker, again to give himself a better chance to save a four. Wouldn't you really like to be as proficient as this out of the sand? "Sure," you say, "but I'll never be able to play out of sand like a pro, just like I'll never be able to consistently bust a drive 280 yards down the middle." Well, here's where I disagree with you. *Sand play is the one area where any amateur can improve to near-professional level, and do so quickly.* That's because the margin for error is much greater on sand shots than on any other shot. Later in this chapter, I'll explain why this is true.

Granted, you probably will never become quite as proficient out of the sand as Gary Player, Chi Chi Rodriguez, or Seve Ballesteros, because these pros, like the rest on the tour, almost always play more excellently groomed courses, where the sand is very consistent from one hole to the next, so they know how the ball will react every time. Also, since golf is a pro's livelihood, he can afford to spend hours and hours practicing sand shots.

Still, once you learn the easy-to-follow, easy-to-learn techniques contained in this chapter, I'm confident that you will quickly make astounding improvement. You may not hit the ball close to the hole every time, but you will be able to step up to any normal bunker shot with the total confidence that you'll make a good recovery. Even if you face an extra-tough stance or lie, or both, with your new arsenal of techniques you'll *always* know you can at the very least put the ball on the putting surface. I ask each of you as individual readers, how much will this degree of ability in the sand help your score during the course of a round? Enough to go to work on it, don't you agree?

There is another great benefit to becoming an excellent sand player: *You can become much more aggressive in going for the flag with your iron shots.* The golfer who dreads being in a trap will never shoot at a flag that's on the right-rear of a green, say, with a bunker guarding the right side of the green. He'll always leave himself a 40-foot putt or even pull the approach shot entirely off the green. With your newfound bunker play skills, you'll know you can shoot closer to the flag, because even if you do put it in the bunker, you'll have a good shot at getting the ball up and down in two. End result: a lot more greens hit with the ball in makeable putt range.

I hope I've convinced you of the value of top-quality sand play, and provided you with the confidence that you can become a really fine sand player. With that, let's move on and talk about the right equipment.

Picking the Right Sand Wedge

Without question, having the right sand wedge can make bunker play immeasurably easier. Yet many amateurs really don't know what to look for in a good sand club. So let's take a moment to explain what you should be looking for.

As stated in the previous chapter, the sand wedge usually carries 55 degrees of loft, as compared with the pitching wedge, which features about 50 degrees of loft. However, there is much more that's different in the design of the sand wedge when compared to the pitching wedge than the mere difference in loft. The most obvious difference is in the design of the *flange* of the sand wedge. It is much broader and thicker than the flange of the pitching wedge or any other iron, giving it more heft, which helps facilitate getting through the sand on blast shots.

As you can clearly see from the accompanying photograph, the sand wedge (right) features more *loft* than the pitching wedge (left).

The most important difference in the sand wedge, however, is the amount of *bounce* built into the flange. *Bounce* means the degree to which the back or rear edge of the flange lies below the leading edge of the flange, when the clubshaft is held in a perfectly vertical position. The sand wedge is the only club in the bag that has this bounce feature built into the flange. The purpose of bounce is to allow the flange to glide through the sand like a knife through butter. Without this bounce, the leading edge would dig into the sand, behind the ball, muffling the shot and perhaps leaving the ball in the bunker.

Sand wedges are made with wider or narrower soles and greater or lesser degrees of bounce. You should select a sand wedge based on the type of sand that predominates on the course or courses you play most often. If your course has deep, soft, heavy sand, you'll find that a large-flanged club with lots of bounce will ride nicely through the sand and make your recoveries much simpler.

You must be careful if the sand is shallower and lighter so that the flange hits the sand trap's hard base. If the sand is thin, a large-flanged club with lots of bounce will bounce too much; it could bounce right off the base of the sand and hit the ball, so that the shot ends up flying over the green. If this is the type of sand at your home course, go for a more compact blade that features a narrower sole and a couple of degrees less bounce.

A word now on the "third" or "lofted" wedges. These clubs have the most loft of all, usually in the 60-degree range but sometimes having even more. They are basically designed to pop the ball out of heavy greenside rough. Notice that, as a rule, the typical third wedge carries much less bounce than a normal sand wedge does, if it carries any bounce at all. This feature, coupled with its very high loft, leads me to recommend that you limit your sand shots with the lofted wedge to only the shortest greenside bunker shots.

Basic Greenside Bunker Techniques

Let's start off by showing you how to play the basic evergreen sand shot. This is the shot the PGA Tour player thinks he can hole out—and the one you will soon feel you can hit within one-putt range every time. This is where your ball is in the middle of the trap so that the lie is fairly flat; the sand is of medium depth; the lie is good (almost all of the ball is above the surface of the sand); you are between 40 and 60 feet from the hole; and you have ample (20 feet or more) green to work with.

The first step toward playing this shot is to wriggle your feet down into the sand, to give you a secure base for your swing. In a sense, *The Rules of Golf* almost lets you "cheat" a little bit when playing a bunker shot. Why do I say this? Well, as you wriggle your feet in, at the same time you are actually assessing the depth and firmness of the sand. If the sand is very deep and soft, so that your feet go down well below the surface, you'll want to hit the shot with a little more force than if your wriggling determines that the sand is shallow and firm. If this is the case, you'll want to take a slightly shorter, less forceful swing.

Always remember to think opposites in the sand. The harder the sand, the easier you swing; the softer and deeper the sand, the harder you must hit the shot.

A word of caution here regarding digging your feet into the sand. While you're allowed to wriggle your feet in and at the same time determine the sand's depth, you may not dig down to judge the depth, then step back and refill the holes you've made to the depth you'd really like for your stance. This rebuilding of your stance will be penalized in either stroke or match play.

You should assume a fairly wide stance for the basic bunker shot, with the distance between your heels about the width of your shoulders. This is a little different from what you may have heard in the past, that you should use a very narrow stance for sand shots. I disagree because the narrow stance encourages a narrow swing arc, in which you pick up the club with a sharp early wrist cock and then drive the club steeply down into the sand. I believe you'll hit much better sand shots if you create a wide swing arc rather than a narrow, abrupt one. Why is this? Because the wider arc is also a shallower arc, which means you will take out a lesser amount of sand through the ball. The less sand you can take, the more control and backspin you'll be able to put on the ball. So take a fairly wide

When playing the basic greenside bunker shot, be sure to *wriggle* your feet down into the sand.

stance and point both toes out slightly. This will help you to turn your hips as I recommend during the swing.

From a normal lie, play the ball opposite your left heel as you would for a full shot. Your weight should be evenly distributed, 50 percent on each foot. Your stance for the basic, medium-length sand shot should be open about 20 degrees to your target. This will create a swing plane that's outside-in, which makes the ball pop out of the sand quickly with some left-to-right cut-spin on the ball for extra bite. Keep in mind that the more open your stance, the higher and softer the ball will come out; the more square you are to the target line, the farther the ball will travel, given the same force of swing while taking the same amount of sand. So for a very short sand shot, open your stance a bit more than 20 degrees. For a longer sand shot (over 60 feet to the hole), the stance should be only slightly open, say 10 degrees.

One way in which the greenside bunker shot differs from a normal fairway shot is that you want to make sure the clubface stays open through and past impact, which allows the club to glide through the sand rather than dig. To this end, grip the club in a weaker than normal position with your left hand. Your left thumb should be straight atop the shaft in the twelve o'clock position, and instead of seeing two knuckles on that hand as in the regular grip, you should be able to see just one knuckle. Meanwhile, the clubface is lying well open at address.

Another adjustment in your grip is that you should choke down on the club about an inch more than normal, so that you can actually see about 2 inches at the end of the grip above the last finger of your left hand. The reason you need to choke down is to compensate for the fact that you've wriggled your feet into the sand about one inch below the sand's surface. If you didn't choke down, the tendency would be for you to hit too far behind the ball and land the ball well short of the hole.

Once you wriggle your feet in, hover the club an inch or so above the sand and an inch behind the ball.

Swing the club back slowly with the left arm in control, creating a relatively wide swing arc. Let the wrists gradually cock, or set,

On basic bunker shots, let the *left* arm control the backswing.

during the backswing, but do not consciously create a severe early wrist cock as has often been advised.

The length of the backswing depends on the length of the shot. I recommend that you always pick out a spot that is about one and a half inches behind the ball. Ignore the ball itself and focus on that spot where you want the flange to contact the sand. Some players vary how much sand they take behind the ball depending on the length of the shot, but to me this is too complicated and demanding. It's much easier to adjust the length of the backswing, while keeping the distance you hit behind the ball constant.

Once you've reached the top, you create acceleration of the clubhead by actively driving your hips in counterclockwise fashion, while also pulling down strongly with your left arm and shoulder. As you pull down with your left side, you must keep your right wrist locked into a flexed-back position in order to keep the clubhead from rolling over through impact. A key thought to help you with this is to think of keeping your right heel pad ahead of the right-hand fingers as the club drives through the sand. This lock of the right wrist eliminates the most common flaw in sand play—trying to scoop the ball up and out by breaking the wrists forward. The usual result of this error is that the clubhead enters the sand far too early, so you leave the ball in the bunker.

Remember my three swing keys of *set, drive, and lock* for the basic sand shot. Set the right wrist gradually into a bent-back position as you swing back from the ball; drive the left hip to create acceleration while pulling down firmly with the left arm; and lock the right wrist back through impact to prevent any scooping action of the clubhead. You're on your way to better bunker play already.

Why Sand Shots Are Easy: A Greater Margin for Error

Let me stop for a moment here to point out exactly why the sand shot from a normal lie is really an easy shot. You have a much greater margin for error in terms of where the club contacts the sand than you have in contacting the ball on a fairway shot. You see, you can hit a normal 50-foot bunker shot a little "fat" or a little "thin," and still be okay.

Let's say, on this 50-foot shot, that you've set up to contact the

Driving your hips in a counterclockwise direction on the downswing is paramount to properly executing the basic bunker shot.

sand one and a half inches behind the ball. If you hit it just right, the ball will come out of the sand high and soft, carry most of the way to the hole, take two bounces before the backspin takes effect, then stop dead. However, you make a slight error and contact the sand two inches behind the ball. In effect, you've hit the shot a half-inch "fat." But look at the result: Instead of carrying most of the way, the shot will only fly a little shorter because more sand between club and ball has had a muffling effect. However, because a sand shot that's hit heavy carries less backspin, the ball will run farther, so that the total distance is nearly the same as if you've nipped the shot perfectly. The shot will still finish relatively close to the hole.

On the other side of the coin, suppose you "thin" the shot a half inch, so that your flange hits the sand only one inch behind the ball. Because there's little sand resistance between club and ball, the shot will come out as if it's going too far. However, when you take this little sand, the ball will be loaded with backspin. The end result is that the shot may fly all the way to the hole, take one big bounce, but then back up a couple of feet, so that it still finishes pretty close to the cup.

So do you see now how the physics are on your side, even if you make a slight mistake in where you contact the sand? Slightly heavy shots carry shorter but run farther; slightly thin shots carry farther but have extra backspin.

Now that you understand this secret and you know the mechanics of the sand shot, you're only a practice session or two from becoming a much-improved sand player. And you'll be able to smile to yourself when you've hit a slight miss from the sand that still finishes relatively near the hole, and your opponent says, "Great shot!"

Let's now prepare you for all those specialty sand shots you'll need when the stance and/or the lie are unusual—and also show you how to play from fairway bunkers.

The Shot from Hard Sand

Quite often, and particularly on courses where the maintenance is less than optimum, you'll face a bunker shot where the ball is lying well, but the sand is very shallow—that is, there is very little cushion above the actual base of the trap. You can determine the depth and hardness of the sand pretty much just by walking up to the ball, and you will definitely be able to assess it as you assume your stance.

The shot from hard sand can be a little bit deceiving because the ball will generally be lying well. Assuming you have a flat lie in the middle of the trap as in the basic bunker shot I've discussed, it will look like an easy shot. The difficulty lies in the tendency for the flange of the sand wedge to bounce when it contacts the hard base just behind the ball. Instead of gliding evenly through the sand, the club can bounce up and contact the ball itself, hitting it well past the hole and perhaps over the green into more trouble. To prevent this from happening, you'll need to make some simple adjustments to your basic sand shot technique.

First, assume the same fairly wide stance as in the normal sand shot. You won't be able to wriggle your feet in as much because the sand is thin, but try to make sure your stance is secure enough to support a full backswing turn without slipping. Keep your weight on the balls of your feet so that you're centered rather than leaning forward or back. Position the ball opposite your left heel, as for a normal sand shot, and, as usual, pick a spot an inch and a half behind the ball where you want to make contact.

The key difference in your setup for this shot is that you must set your hands two inches farther ahead at address than normal. This means the clubface will be virtually square as opposed to laid open. This also sets you up to descend a little more sharply into the sand behind the ball, so that the flange will dig in a little more rather than bounce.

Use a slow rhythm as you swing the club back, again allowing your wrists to hinge naturally and gradually rather than cocking them early. Coming down, create acceleration with your hips while swinging your left arm down firmly. If anything, on this shot you must be even more certain to lock the right wrist back so that the hands lead the club sharply down into the sand.

Because you're making a more downward blow, the ball will shoot out a little lower than for the basic sand shot and will bounce a bit farther before the backspin makes it bite. For this reason, you'll actually need to take a slightly shorter swing to cover the distance than you would from a good lie in medium-deep sand.

The "Ice Cream Scoop" Shot

You've probably all experienced that sinking feeling after hitting an iron shot that finds a bunker, when you realize that not only are you trapped, but that the ball has buried itself in deep sand. Particularly if the ball is still 20 to 30 feet from the edge of the green and the bunker is fairly deep, you may even be almost resigned to wasting a shot just to get out of that horrible lie, then hitting a second sand shot to actually reach the putting surface. Well, those days of leaving a buried ball in the bunker should be over, because you're about to learn my favorite specialty, the *ice cream scoop shot*.

The situation is that the ball is lying in its own crater, almost completely buried in sand. Ordinarily you'd figure that even if you do manage to gouge the ball out, it will carry no backspin and probably will run over the green. However, the scoop shot enables

The *buried* lie in a bunker looks like this.

The number one
backswing key for
playing the ice cream
scoop shot is to *pick
up* the club abruptly on
a steep angle.

you to not only get the ball out, but actually put some spin on the ball so that it stays reasonably close to the hole.

Your technique for this shot is really quite a bit different from what we've discussed so far. First, take a slightly narrower stance (about 3 inches narrower than normal) because in this instance you want a steeper backswing and downswing. Second, play the ball farther back in your stance than normal, between the center of your stance and the inside of your right heel. Meanwhile, keep your hands in their normal address position. This means they will be ahead of the ball and the clubface will be *closed* rather than open. Your weight should favor your left side, with about 70 percent on your left foot to encourage a downward blow. Hover the club just behind the ball; for this shot only you'll want to strike the sand just one inch behind it. Finally, grip the club with your normal left-hand grip—that is, with your thumb at one o'clock rather than twelve o'clock as described for the basic sand shot.

The "scoop" is the one shot in which you pick up the club abruptly with a quick wrist cock. In starting down, create acceleration by simultaneously rotating the hips in a counterclockwise direction and pulling down strongly with your left arm. As the clubhead enters the sand, make your left elbow wing or fly out away from your body; this winging action makes the clubhead take out a short, deep scoop of sand rather than the long, thin divot for a basic sand shot. This short, deep scoop is really shaped a lot like a scoop of ice cream.

As you wing your left elbow to take out that scoop of sand, the face of your sand wedge will be moving from a square, hooded position into an open one. This opening of the face very effectively works the flange *underneath* the ball, even though it was buried. So when this shot is properly executed, the ball will pop out relatively softly. Not only can you hit the ball out, you can get it close.

Go out to a practice bunker some evening. Drop a dozen balls into the bunker and bury them. Then practice my scoop technique. It shouldn't take long before you see that this seemingly impossible shot is really quite easy to play.

Be sure to "wing"
your left elbow when
playing the ice cream
scoop shot.

**The Downhill
Bunker Shot**

Here is another specialty sand situation in which a few adjustments will make a scary shot quite manageable.

Your ball is lying in the back part of a bunker. This means that not only is it resting on a downhill lie, but you have almost all of the bunker to carry before you get to the green. Let's say the total distance of the shot is 60 feet, with 40 feet of sand, bank, and fringe to carry, and just 20 feet of green to work with. The obvious difficulties of this shot are that the ball will be coming off a downhill lie, which will make it fly lower; yet it must carry to the green and stop quickly if it's to finish near the hole.

Your first step to conquering the downhill sand shot is to wriggle your feet very securely into the downhill slope of sand. It's very easy to slip during the swing when the sand isn't level. Make sure your footing is really secure, with your weight shaded more on your lower foot.

Both your stance and the blade should be wide open for this shot. Each of these adjustments contributes to hitting the ball higher and softer to compensate for the downhill lie. Grip the club with the left hand in the weak or twelve o'clock position discussed earlier, to help keep the clubface open through impact. The ball should be positioned farther back than normal, at approximately the center of the stance. Aim the flange of the club to hit an inch and a half behind the ball as usual.

In executing the swing, take the club back in a smooth, wide arc with a gradual rather than an abrupt wrist cock. You'll need a little less backswing to cover the distance to the hole than you would from a flat lie. Start the downswing by clearing the left hip, while keeping the right wrist locked back.

Your key to playing this shot successfully is to swing down along the slope through and past impact. Really make an effort to stay down. The fatal flaw in playing the downhill sand shot is a last-second attempt to lift the ball up, resulting in a line-drive "skull." Stay down and swing with the slope. Your open stance and open clubface will counteract the degree of downhill slope so that the ball rises nicely and with good backspin.

On downhill lies, swing *down* along the slope.

The Uphill Lie Under the Lip

Here's a special situation which I think is really easy to play, once you know the correct adjustments to make.

Your ball is on the upslope of a bunker, just a couple of feet back from the lip. Since you are in the side of the bunker nearest the green, you have little sand and fringe to carry and plenty of green to work with. Because the ball is being hit off an upslope, there is a definite tendency to pop the ball high in the air and leave this shot well short of the hole. So my first piece of advice is to plan to hit the shot twice as hard as if it were the same distance from a flat lie. If the ball is 30 feet from the pin, play it as if it were 60 feet.

In assuming your address, lean into the slope rather than along with it as for the downhill lie. This means that most of your weight is on your front foot. Leaning into the slope will help counteract the tendency to pop the ball straight up. Assume your normal fairly wide stance.

Also, as you can see from the accompanying illustration, the stance and clubface are only a shade open. This is because the upslope of the sand will provide more than enough lift to the shot.

Your swing mechanics for the uphill shot are almost exactly the same as for the basic shot. You must take a slow, wide backswing arc with a gradual wrist cock, an accelerating downswing keyed by the rotary action of the hips, and a strong pull-down with the left arm while keeping the right wrist locked back. Aim to splash the sand no more than one and a half inches behind the ball. (The only difference in the swing involves a tempo change. Make sure to swing aggressively and, unless the green is sloping away from you, try to fly the ball all the way to the hole. The ball will fly high and drop almost straight down, so that it stops quickly upon landing.)

Fairway Bunker Tactics and Techniques

Let's complete this chapter with some instruction on how to get the most out of your shots from fairway bunkers. The fairway bunker shot is really a separate category from greenside sand shots. This is because from a fairway bunker, you want to contact the ball first

On uphill lies, set the
stance and the
clubface a shade *open*.

as opposed to slapping the sand behind the ball in a greenside bunker.

Before we get into the mechanics of fairway bunker play, let's get our strategic thoughts in order. Here's an example in which your tee shot has landed in the middle of a fairway bunker, 175 yards from the hole. The ball is lying relatively well; however, there's a moderately steep grassy wall or lip over which you must hit the ball.

Naturally, you'd like to knock this shot onto the green. Ordinarily, let's say the distance would call for a 4-iron. However, you have a problem in that you must take enough loft to get over that lip first. So before you set up to the shot, take a careful look at the lip and decide whether the club you need in order to reach the green also has enough loft to clear the lip. (I find it very helpful to stand to the side so you can more easily assess the distance from the ball to the lip and the trajectory the ball must take off on to safely clear it.) If you feel you'd be gambling with a 4-iron, select a lofted club that you know will hit the ball over the lip.

When hitting from fairway sand, you always want to contact the ball first. The only exception to this is when the ball is buried. Then you may be forced to simply blast back into the fairway. As a rule, though, the ball doesn't bury as much in a fairway bunker, since you usually hit into them with a long club such as a driver, so that the ball descends on a low trajectory.

Keeping in mind the cardinal rule to get the ball safely over the lip, you've now selected a club and are ready to play the shot. Grip the club normally. Assume the same width of stance you would take with this club from the fairway. Your shoulders, hips, knees, and feet should all be parallel to your target line. Wriggle your feet well into the sand until you feel secure that you won't slip. Because your feet are below the surface, choke down on the club an extra inch, the same as described for greenside sand shots.

Since you want to make sure to contact the ball first, I recommend you play the ball just a touch back from normal—say one ball width back from a line drawn opposite your left heel. This helps ensure that the blade contacts the ball before the sand.

Your swing doesn't change much from the mechanics for a normal fairway shot. There's no need to cock the wrists abruptly or pick up the club in an exaggerated fashion. Swing the club back in a wide arc and let your wrists hinge gradually. The main difference in the swing is that you should feel as if your arms are doing most of the work. The reason for this is that you don't want quite as much lower-body movement, since it's easy to slip on longer shots from fairway bunkers.

From the top, feel like you're making a strong downward pulling action with the left arm and shoulder. Although you won't follow through quite as fully as normal because of the resistance of the sand beyond impact, definitely try for a normal follow-through to avoid any chance of quitting on the shot.

With proper execution, the ball should fly fairly low and straight. It's a good idea to aim for an open area of the green so that if you do catch the ball a little thin, it can still run onto the green.

One final tip on club selection: Assuming you don't have any problem getting the ball over the lip, it's wise to select one club longer than you normally would, say a 5-iron instead of a 6. This is because choking down on the club and limiting your lower body action lessen the total distance of the shot by about one club.

Well, I believe you're ready now, with just a little practice, to become a master of the sand game.

**RITSON'S
REVIEW**

Basic Bunker Play Techniques
- Assume a relatively wide stance for normal sand shots.
- Grip weak with the left hand in those situations where you want to keep the clubface open.
- Aim one and a half inches behind the ball from greenside bunkers.
- Make a low, slow backswing with a gradual wrist cock for normal bunker shots.

Sophisticated Sand Play Techniques
- For the buried lie, play the ice cream scoop shot.
- Swing down the slope on downhill bunker shots.
- Hit twice as hard as you think you need to from bunker lies on the upslope.
- From fairway bunkers, always take ample loft to clear the lip in front of you.

6 | WINNING IN THE WIND

Knowing how to battle the breeze will make you a more complete player

The vast majority of amateur golfers seem to equate a round played in a 25-mile-per-hour wind with the pleasure they'll get from their next visit to the dentist. All they can envision are tee shots blown into deep rough or out of bounds, well-struck iron shots being held up in a tempest and burying in a front bunker, and downwind pitch shots scuttling over the greens into trouble. And at the end of the round, they see a scorecard totaling as many as a dozen strokes higher than they might have carded if the conditions had been normal.

If you are one of the many amateurs who falls into this negative thought pattern, I'd like to convince you to make an attitude adjustment. The wind is not some additional burden you are being forced to deal with on certain days. It is an integral part of the game of golf. You won't improve as a wind player until you accept the tenet that wind is a factor to consider on every golf shot you play, just like the yardage, the lie of the ball, the position of the pin, and so on.

Granted, the wind will have a varying amount of influence on your game, depending on what part of the country you reside in. If you live in Florida as I do, or in areas such as Texas or the Plains states, you know that on most days the wind will have quite a say in how you'll play your shots. Not only does the wind tend to blow consistently in these regions, but the terrain is relatively level and there are few tall trees to block the wind. I'm so used to playing in windy conditions by now that I sometimes get thrown off kilter on those days when there's no wind to factor into my shotmaking.

If you live in the Northeast or the near-midwestern part of the country, the wind may not be quite as dominant a factor. Many of the courses are somewhat hilly and usually have trees lining most of the fairways, so many shots will be protected from the wind's influence. Still, wind can be a devilish factor on these "protected" courses. It can swirl in different directions and mislead you as to how it will affect the ball. A perfect example of this is the par-three twelfth hole at Augusta National in Augusta, Georgia, home of The Masters. The hole, just 155 yards over Rae's Creek to a shallow green, sits in a low area of the course among stately pines and is the centerpiece of a three-hole stretch known as "Amen Corner." Because the wind is so fickle and even the tiniest misjudgment can prove fatal, the world's greatest golfers consider this the toughest tournament par three anywhere.

So even on hilly and treed courses, the wind will have some effect on your shots. And even if you do live in a less windy section of the country, the wind is really a universal factor in months like March, April, October, and November.

Learn to Welcome the Wind

Let me tell you about my own attitude about playing in the wind. I love it. My mind is constantly working throughout the round, with the wind coming from varying directions and/or at a different strength from the day before. Every hole and every shot plays subtly differently, and that's good. I find it fascinating and challenging to face a shot of, say, 150 yards one day where it's a soft, floating 8-iron shot, and then see it as a crisp, three-quarter 4-iron shot on the next. The wind adds tremendous variety to the shot-making demands each hole can offer.

Once you embrace this productive attitude that the wind is one of the integral challenges of the game of golf, rather than a hindrance toward shooting a good score, you've made the first step toward becoming a better wind player. Not only will you learn how to use the wind to your advantage in certain situations and minimize its negative effects in others, you'll also realize that on certain really windy days, the golf course is going to play much tougher than others. There may be days when a course with a par of 72 may really be playing to a par of 75. If you realize in advance that your score is likely to go up about three shots, and make up your mind to give each shot your best thought as well as your best swing, believe me, you'll end up scoring much closer to your norm than your opponents.

Let's talk about both the mental and physical aspects that go into improved wind play. Regarding certain shotmaking situations, particularly in crosswinds, I will provide you with both basic and advanced techniques. Always base your wind play shotmaking decisions on how confident you feel in your own swing. If you are comfortable with the tee shot advocated in the advanced technique, go for it. If not, using the basic wind techniques will still prove very helpful to your game.

Become a Good Wind Watcher

The first part of becoming a good windy-day player is to learn to gauge the wind accurately. Not only do you need to judge its strength, but also how it's likely to affect the particular shot you're about to play.

If you're on a relatively flat, open hole with no protection from the breeze, it's pretty simple to estimate the wind. You can simply toss some grass in the air and obtain a feel for the wind's direction and strength. If you're approaching the green, you can also observe the way the flag is blowing. This information should give you a good idea of the shot you should play and the club you'll need.

Oftentimes, though, the strength and direction of the wind will be a little tougher to judge. For example, you may be hitting a drive from a tree-enclosed tee out to a more open fairway area (or to a wind-whipped green on a par-three hole). Just because you don't feel much wind where you stand doesn't mean it's not out there. Remember also that the wind will have its greatest effect on the ball near the end of its flight, when its forward momentum is nearly spent.

In situations such as this, where the tee is enclosed, three things can help:

1. Observe any trees near the landing area of the upcoming shot, or the flag if it's a par-three hole. Any movement you see there will be a better indicator than what you feel on the tee.

2. Recall other holes you've already played that run in the same direction as the upcoming one, and how the wind affected them. If you haven't yet played a hole in the direction of the upcoming one, assess how the wind blew on the holes you played in the opposite direction.

3. If you're not the first player to hit, observe your playing partners' shots carefully; particularly if they hit their shots pretty similarly to your own, you can pick up some very valuable information here. Be alert.

In addition to determining the strength and direction of the wind, keep in mind the combined effect of the wind with the lay of the land on a particular hole. For example, if you're playing a downhill hole from a slightly elevated tee, the ball will be in the air longer than normal. Thus, a wind from any direction will have much more effect on it. An uphill shot, conversely, will stay closer to the ground throughout its trajectory and will not be affected as much.

When in Doubt, Take More Club

Before getting into specific wind-shot situations, I'd like you to remember this important general observation: The biggest mistake I see amateurs make when playing in a substantial wind is to take too little club on their approach shots. This holds true no matter from what direction the wind is coming, but it's most particularly evident on shots played into the wind.

In a strong headwind, the worst thing you can do is select a club that you must hit perfectly to get to the pin, then try to hit the shot hard. Here's why: First, the harder you swing, the more backspin you'll apply to the ball. And the more backspin you put on the shot, the more it will rise or "upshoot" into a headwind. After hanging in the air seemingly forever, it will fall well short of your target. You will actually get more distance into the wind with a smoother swing that puts less backspin on the ball.

Second, whenever you make a big swing into a heavy wind, it's much harder to keep your balance, which is so vital to making straight contact. It's crucial to swing within yourself in windy conditions to give yourself the best possible chance to make a straight hit.

As a general rule of thumb, you should take one less lofted club for every 10 miles per hour of wind against you. A 20-mile-per-hour wind warrants two clubs stronger than normal. And don't hesitate to go three or four clubs longer than normal in really strong gusts. Take enough club so you can make a nice, compact, three-quarter swing that enables you to keep your balance for good contact, while at the same time keeping the ball lower for better control into the breeze.

When hitting into a crosswind from either direction, remember that this will affect the distance as well as the direction of the shot. A straight shot that's being pushed from one side by the wind will tend to get knocked down a little faster than usual. So remember that you usually need one club extra in crosswinds as well.

Downwind shots into the greens can be played several different ways, and thus it's harder to categorize how to make your club selection based solely on the strength of the wind. Keep in mind, however, that it's just as important to maintain your balance downwind as it is upwind. So while you might use one club shorter than normal, rarely if ever should you force a downwind shot with a big swing and a lot more loft.

To sum up regarding windy-day club selection, I recommend that whenever you're in doubt about what club to choose to approach the green, go with the stronger club and the controlled swing. In fact, next time you play in the wind, figure out how many times you actually hit the ball past pin-high using this approach. If you were past the hole more often than short of it, you're definitely an exception to the rule.

Let's talk about the best way to play various types of windy-weather shots, starting with the tee shot. There are three basic driving situations to consider: into the wind, with the wind, and in crosswinds.

Swing Easy in a Headwind

No doubt, the into-the-wind tee shot, particularly on longer holes, is a shot that rates high on any handicap player's problem list. It's so easy to succumb to the urge to hit hard in an attempt to make up for the distance the wind is likely to take away.

You must be mentally disciplined when teeing off into the wind, because you need to do exactly the opposite of what it feels like you should do—that is, swing easily instead of hard. Visualizing an on-balance erect finish as you set up to the ball will encourage a smooth swing.

As I mentioned earlier, the harder you swing at the ball, the more backspin the club will impart to it. This is true with the driver as well as with the shorter irons. The harder you swing at the driver and the more backspin you apply to it, the more the head-wind works under the ball, pushing it farther upward in its flight. The higher it flies, the more it hangs before dropping steeply to the ground so that it gets little or no roll.

Into a strong wind, you want to hit a tee shot with a relatively low, boring flight and less backspin so that the wind never works its way under the ball. The best way to obtain this dartlike trajectory is to tee the ball higher and swing the driver easier.

Teeing the ball higher encourages a slightly flatter swing plane. In addition to aiding you in putting a touch of draw spin on the ball, which is helpful, the flatter plane brings the clubhead into the ball at a more level angle. This helps make the ball bore into the wind as opposed to a more up-and-down arc, which can give you unwanted backspin. So tee the ball just a quarter-inch higher than normal.

In a headwind, see yourself finishing "tall" before you swing.

Lift Your Launch Angle When the Wind Is at Your Back

All players look forward to those tee shots where the wind is at their backs, so they can really give the ball a ride. The problem is, sometimes players try so hard to slug the ball that they mishit it into trouble bordering the fairway.

While you certainly want to take advantage of a helping breeze, you still need to play a good, solid shot. What you want to do is launch your tee shot at a higher angle than normal, so you get more air under the ball early and a bigger boost from the wind. You need only make a few small adjustments in your setup and swing to get added height.

First, tee the ball just a fraction higher than you normally do. Yes, I know this is the same advice as for the into-the-wind shot. However, with the wind you should also play the ball about 2 inches forward of its normal position, so that it's opposite your left instep rather than the left heel. Also, distribute your weight so it's a little more on your right foot than normal. From this position, make your normal driver swing, concentrating on making a slow takeaway and keeping your head behind the ball.

These adjustments will cause you to contact the ball with your driver moving into the upswing as opposed to level to the ground. This will effectively add 2 to 3 degrees' loft to the clubface at impact. The higher launch angle can easily give you 20 or 30 extra yards on your drive, even more with a really strong wind.

One final tip on downwind drives. If there is a near gale blowing behind you (say 25 miles per hour or more), tee off with your 3-wood rather than a driver. With this much wind behind you, getting the ball up in the air quickly will more than make up for the normal difference in yardage between the driver and the 3-wood.

Crosswind Driving: The Correct Strategy

I'm convinced that the safest way to play your tee shots in a crosswind is to aim your ball to the side of the target from which the wind is blowing, then let the wind work it back. For example, if you note a breeze of about 15 miles per hour from the left, aim about 15

When the wind is at your back, play the ball more *forward* in your stance.

yards left of the center of the fairway, then simply let the wind drift the ball back.

In addition, you may recall, too, that in Chapter Three I recommended the more sophisticated methods of playing a draw in a right-to-left crosswind or a fade in a left-to-right crosswind, as a means of picking up extra distance. This is an excellent tactic on long holes that offer plenty of driving room, provided you are confident that you can work the ball. Using the swing principles outlined in that chapter, aim the ball well left of the target in a left-to-right breeze, or well right of it when the wind sweeps in from the right. The long draw or long fade that you hit can give you an extra 20 yards or more.

Iron Play in the Wind

Let's move on now to discuss the various tactics that apply to your approach shots in windy conditions. You'll notice that for most golfers, I will not suggest the same shots into the greens as I might from the tee. Generally speaking, the more distance you can get off the tee, the better. Also, you'll usually have some leeway in the landing area for a tee shot. However, in playing the irons you must control both distance and direction; thus you must learn to be more creative and strategically smart in your shot selection.

Into-the-Wind Punch

On the vast majority of approach shots where you are playing into a strong headwind, I recommend that you play a controlled, three-quarter punch shot for maximum accuracy.

Let's say you are 140 yards from a flag positioned more or less in the center of a green which is bunkered on the sides but not in front. Ordinarily, you might play a 7-iron in this situation. However, there's a stiff breeze against you, so it's time to play the punch shot.

The first maxim in playing a punch with an iron is to always select a stronger club than normal. By taking plenty of stick, you're more likely to make a smoother swing in the wind and strike the ball solidly. The easier swing will also allow you to put less backspin on

To successfully hit a penetrating punch shot into the wind, play the ball in the center of your stance.

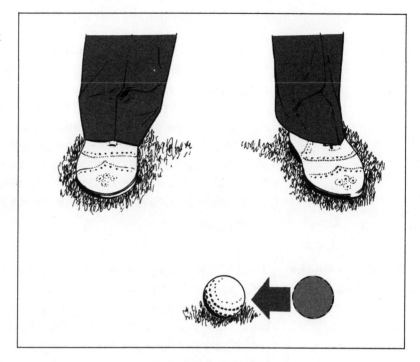

the ball, so that it bores through the wind rather than upshooting. As with the driver, you will actually be getting the most out of the club with what feels like a lesser swing.

Once you've picked out a club, set up with the ball located in the center of your stance. Choke down on the grip about 1 inch. Your hands should be 3 to 4 inches ahead of the ball, with the clubface slightly hooded (tilted slightly toward the ground) and the leading edge perpendicular to your target. Keep about 70 percent of your weight on your left side at address.

In executing the punch, let your arms control the shot. Push the club away from the ball with your left arm and the club moving as one unit. Swing back no farther than the three-quarter position, keeping your wrists firm and with less weight moving onto your right side than normal. Your start-down should feel as if you are pulling straight down, as if tolling a bell, with your left arm. To keep the ball low, make the hands chase the club into the follow-through, so you finish pointing the club directly at the target. The lower the finish, the lower the shot.

Although the ball will start off low, keep in mind that if the ball has been struck solidly, it will rise and carry a little more than you might think. This is true because the headwind will work under the backspinning ball to some degree. For this reason, you may need to carry the into-the-wind punch a little farther than you think, since it won't roll that far after landing. For the 140-yard shot described, you may need to carry the shot 125 yards, or about to the front fringe, allowing for some 15 yards of run after the shot lands. The stronger the headwind, the less the ball will run.

Punch It with the Wind, Too

There's lots of debate on the subject of how to cope with iron shots with the wind at your back. One school of thought says you should try to hit the irons high to take advantage of the wind and to land the ball on the green as softly as possible. To do this, you would play the ball an inch forward of your normal position and keep your upper body behind the ball, so you sweep the ball off the ground.

Whenever the green is guarded by a front bunker so that you must carry the ball to the green, the high downwind iron is a must. However, most often the greenside bunkering is on the sides, allowing you to play a lower shot that runs onto the green. I believe this lower, punched shot will prove to be the percentage play in downwind situations for two reasons:

1. It's easier to control the distance of the lower downwind shot, so you reduce the chances of flying the ball over the green.
2. The punch shot is technically a simpler shot to hit. (With the high shot and its sweeping swing action, you run more risk of hitting the shot "fat" so that it ends up way short.)

For the downwind punch in a moderate-strength wind, you'll probably use one more lofted club than normal. Assume your normal grip and play the ball just ahead of the stance's center point.

Your hands should be ahead of the ball, with most of your weight on the left side. Make a one-piece takeaway, with your left arm and the clubshaft going back together. Swing up to a three-quarter position, keeping the wrists firm. Then pull the club straight down with your left arm and side while keeping the body relatively still.

For the downwind punch, you don't need to keep the shot quite as low as when into the wind (remember that a wind behind you will also work to knock the ball down slightly). So instead of pointing the clubshaft to the target at the finish, allow your hands to finish a little higher—say just reaching the level of your left shoulder.

In planning the downwind punch, remember that the ball will land "hotter" than it will into the wind. So instead of landing the ball around the front edge of the green, plan on pitching it 10 to 20 yards short and letting it run to the flag. The less loft you use, the farther you should land the ball short.

You'll find this downwind punch a very reliable shot to play. Both the into-the-wind and downwind punch shots do require some feel and practice. The best way to obtain this feel is to go out to your home course on a breezy evening when the course is uncrowded. Hit several punch shots to a green into the wind, then go to another hole where you're playing the shot downwind. Observe the carry and roll you get in both situations as well as implementing the setup adjustments for the punch. You'll find this practice very beneficial the next time the wind is really blowing.

Getting It Close in Crosswinds

When playing iron shots in crosswinds, you can take one of two approaches. The basic approach is to play a straight shot, aiming left of the hole in a left-to-right wind and right of the hole in a right-to-left wind. The more advanced method is to draw or fade the ball into the crosswind, with the bend in the shot counteracting the wind's influence.

Most high-handicap players are probably best off playing a straight shot and letting the wind do the work. Other than adjusting your aim correctly for the wind, everything else is standard, so there's less that can go wrong.

When putting on windy days, make sure you stay *rock steady* over the ball.

A low-handicap player who can fade or draw the ball at will is probably best off trying to work the ball against the crosswind, because it does give you the best chance of hitting the ball really close to the hole.

Say the wind is coming from the left and the pin is pretty much centered on the green. If you play a successful straight shot and let the wind blow it back, you can land it a little left of the hole and let it run a bit to the right, so it finishes close. If the pin is tucked left, however, you may have to settle for a little longer putt. The big plus for playing into a crosswind is that the ball's spin fights the wind, so that it flies very straight, then lands very softly because the wind has knocked it down. Therefore, you can shoot for the flag wherever it's located on the green.

The Wind Affects Your Short Game, Too!

Around and on the greens, don't forget that the wind can still influence your shots. Short pitches and chip shots will run a little farther than you might normally expect them to, so allow for it. Likewise, these short shots might pull up a little more quickly than normal when there's a good breeze against you.

When playing lofted pitches into a wind, you have an advantage, particularly when you must lob the ball over a bunker to a tight pin position. You can play a nice firm shot with a wedge, carrying the ball almost to the hole, then watch it stop dead. Make sure to be aggressive and take a little more of a backswing than you might think you'll need.

In a strong wind, putting can present a very delicate challenge. First of all, when it's windy the greens will dry out, making them faster than normal. Also, the wind will have some effect on a ball rolling on the ground as well as in the air. Downwind putts will be superquick, while into the wind you must remember to apply a firmer stroke.

The biggest difficulty of putting in the wind, though, is maintaining your balance throughout the stroke. Even the slightest movement can cause you to mishit the putt, and very few mishit putts hold their line to the cup. So your key for putting in the wind is to stay as solid over the ball as possible. The best way to accomplish this is to widen your stance a good 4 to 6 inches more than normal. Your legs will act like a tripod, giving you a wider base and making you stand a little shorter than normal. Try to keep your head and upper body rock steady throughout the stroke.

RITSON'S REVIEW

Judging the Wind
- Think of wind as a shotmaking challenge rather than a hindrance.
- When the tee is secluded, use the flag or trees in the landing area to judge the wind's strength.
- Watch the wind's effect on your playing partners' shots.
- Downhill shots will be influenced more by the wind.

Windy-Day Swing Thoughts
- Take plenty of club, particularly into wind.
- Assume a wider stance for stability.
- Limit the swing to three-quarter length.

Tee Shot Strategies
- Into wind, tee the ball slightly higher and swing easier.
- With wind, play the ball more forward in the stance.
- In crosswinds, play a straight shot and let the wind bring the ball toward the target.

Approaches in the Wind
- Play the punch into the wind, and when hitting downwind, too, for maximum control.
- Drawing or fading the ball into crosswinds is the best way to get the ball close.

Short Game Thoughts
- Play for more run on downwind pitches and chips.
- Be aggressive when pitching into the wind.
- Remember that wind dries out greens and can influence the roll of the ball.
- Widen your stance to brace yourself on the greens.

7 | BIG SHOTS

Once you learn these trouble shot techniques, no course situation will scare you

It would be wonderful if we played every golf shot from a perfect lie on short fairway grass, with a wide-open angle to the beckoning flag. I hope, given the information you've learned so far about the setup and the swing, and with some diligent practice, you will increase the percentage of shots you play from ideal positions. However, even the world's greatest golfers find their share of trouble. So, logically, you will never be able to play completely trouble-free golf, either.

In this respect, golf is really a lot like life. You may be a very intelligent, well-organized individual who plans the events of the day very carefully, yet this doesn't guarantee that your day will go completely as envisioned. You might get involved in a fender bender on your way to the office. Once there, you may find that a monstrous work assignment has been plopped on your desk with no warning and an impossible deadline. Then you stagger home to find your neighbor's dog has chosen your vegetable garden as the site of an archaeological dig for bones.

To a greater or lesser degree, your golf rounds will ask you to deal with trouble, too. How well you're able to recover from these tough spots on the course will have a big bearing on your end-of-the-day score.

In this chapter, I'll show you how to play some fancy specialty shots so that you can deal with practically any bad lie or tough situation you confront between the tee and the green. In addition to the techniques you'll learn for each shot, remember to look at these challenging situations as positive opportunities rather than invitations to disaster. Hitting one of these shots successfully can give you a mental boost or rattle your opponent, turning the match in your favor. When facing a trouble shot, don't get disheartened for a minute. Many of golf's greatest champions would never have amassed their records if they hadn't become masters of these recovery shots and literally willed their way out of trouble. Arnold Palmer, Tom Watson, and Seve Ballesteros are great trouble players who come quickly to mind.

So put on your positive attitude and get ready to learn how to tackle golf's "big shots."

Shot One—From a Divot

One of the more frustrating moments for the club-level player occurs when he reaches his ball after a fine drive, only to find it resting in a divot hole. The biggest error amateurs make in this situation is that they try to pick the ball cleanly out of the divot. Usually this results in a topped shot. To extricate your ball from a divot hole, you must swing aggressively down and through the ball.

Assume your address position with the ball placed opposite the center of your stance, while keeping your hands well ahead of the clubface and about 75 percent of your weight on your left side. This presets the sharp, descending blow you'll need. Addressing the ball in this manner also decreases the club's natural loft somewhat, so you should take a more lofted club than normal, say a 7-iron instead of a 6.

Make a three-quarter-length backswing in which your arms control the action and your weight shift to the right is less pronounced than normal. Then pull the club down sharply with your left hand

Set your hands well *ahead* of the ball when preparing to hit a recovery shot from a divot hole.

and arm, trusting the loft of the club to get the ball up and out. Your follow-through will be somewhat lower than normal because of the steeper-than-normal contact with the turf.

One caution from fairway divots: If you face a long shot that requires, say, a 2-iron, don't try to be a hero. Take a 4- or 5-iron and use the same aggressive technique described to get the ball as close to the green as possible. You can still save par with a good chip and putt.

Shot Two— Cuppy Lie

All fairways aren't absolutely perfect. There can be quite a few nooks and crannies hidden within that seemingly plush, carpetlike surface. And since a golf ball will obey the law of gravity and search out the ground's lowest point, you'll frequently find yourself in a depression—a "cuppy" fairway lie that prevents you from sweeping the shot.

Your best method of escape in such circumstances is to cut across the ball, hitting it from the side. To accomplish this sideswipe, swing the club back outside the target line and stop at the three-quarter point. Start down by clearing your left hip quickly to the left. This gives your arms room to swing the club freely across the target line. Make sure to hold on firmly with the left hand to ensure that the clubface does not turn over, or close, through impact. The ball should start well left of the target, then fade substantially. So make sure to align your body well left of the target line, and play one club longer than the distance normally requires.

Shot Three— Downhill Lie

Most middle and high handicappers encounter a great deal of trouble with downhill fairway lies. The basic problem the typical player falls into is the mental trap that he must help the ball get up in the air, rather than let the club's natural loft take care of that goal.

If you're struggling with the downhill lie, be sure to assess the degree of downslope. If it's moderate, pick one club shorter than you normally would for the given yardage. On a severe downslope, go two clubs shorter.

Address the ball just behind the center of your stance, which should be slightly open, and lean into the slope. Because of the ball-back position, your hands will be well ahead of the clubhead, causing the effective loft of the club to be decreased. This is the reason it's difficult to get the ball airborne. If you remember to take more loft, you'll eliminate most of this problem.

Swing the club back *outside* the target line when playing a shot from a cuppy lie.

Swing the club back on a fairly upright arc, cocking the wrists a little earlier than you would from a level lie.

To help you maintain balance on the downswing, be sure to make a rotary turn of your hips. (A strong lateral drive with the legs, coupled with the fact that your weight is moving down a slope to begin with, can cause you to lose balance and move past the ball prior to impact.)

On downhill shots,
play the ball *back* more
in your stance.

Even with a nice rotary weight shift, your tendency will be to get ahead of the shot a bit so that the clubface is still a touch open at impact. Your slightly open address position will compensate for this tendency. Through the hitting zone, resist the urge to try to pick the shot. Instead, make the clubhead follow the downslope well beyond contact. Trust the extra loft you've selected to produce a close-to-normal trajectory and roll upon landing.

Shot Four— Uphill Lie

While uphill lies may not cause as much fear as the downhill shot, most club players don't hit the greens from these slopes as often as they should. The main fault here is the tendency to hit well behind the ball because the player sets up with his shoulders parallel with the horizon rather than parallel with the upslope.

The setup is the key to playing the uphill shot successfully. Position your body perpendicular to the slope. This places your head and your body weight more behind the ball than usual. Apply your normal swing technique, with the exception that you should limit the swing to three-quarter length. This will offset the tendency to move off the ball or sway to the right. On the downswing, keep your head still and swing the club up the slope to a high finish.

Because the steep upslope will naturally prevent you from making a full weight transfer onto your left side on the downswing, your hands will turn over more freely than usual through the impact zone. This produces a draw, so align yourself a little right of the flag at address. Finally, because you're set up level to the upslope, the effective loft of the club will be increased at impact. If the slope is steep, take two clubs more than normal. This will help you to swing within yourself, yet fly the ball all the way to the hole.

Shot Five—Ball Above Feet

When you encounter a sidehill lie with the ball well above your feet, the tendency is to pull-hook the shot. However, if you make the proper corrections at address, you'll play this shot much more consistently.

Because the ball is closer to you than it would be from a level lie, compensate by choking down more than normal. As this shortens

On uphill shots,
parallel your shoulders
to the slope.

your swing arc and thus the yardage you'll obtain, always take one club stronger than normal from this lie. Position the ball an inch or two back from its usual position opposite the left heel. Take the club back normally, then start down by clearing your left hip. Keep the tempo smooth and never force the shot.

You'll naturally swing the club on a flatter plane than usual because the ball is above you, and this will cause the shot to draw. So remember to align yourself to the right of the hole and also to allow for a little run on the ball after landing. NOTE: If the pin is tucked just over a bunker, don't try to be fancy; always aim to hit the middle of the green.

Shot Six—Ball Below Feet

A common fault for many amateurs is to come out of their shots early, meaning they lift the upper body out of its original position prior to impact. This causes you to hit shots that are topped or hit thin, and that fly to the right of target. A sidehill lie with the ball below your feet can really intensify this problem. Here's how to handle shots from this challenging lie.

Grip the club at the end of the handle, since the ball is farther away from you than normal. Because this will also create a wider swing arc than usual, take a 5-iron if the shot would ordinarily call for a 4-iron.

As you address the ball from its normal position opposite the left heel, sit down to the shot more than usual, with your knees well flexed and your weight more toward your heels. Concentrate on maintaining this knee flex throughout the swing. Loss of balance by leaning down the slope is the prime cause of mishit shots from this somewhat awkward lie.

Since the ball is below you, your swing plane will naturally be more upright than it would be from a level lie. Therefore, when you make contact at impact, the shot will tend to fade slightly. Aim a few yards to the left of the pin to compensate.

Shot Seven— Tight Lie

Often your ball will stop on a spot in the fairway with a minimal cushion of grass underneath it—a "tight" lie. Amateurs often find

When the ball is above your feet, aim *right* of the target to allow for "draw-flight."

When the ball is below your feet, "sit" down more at address.

this unsettling, particularly if they face a long or medium iron shot to the green. It's not that tough, believe me. In fact, the pros would rather play from a very tight lie than a grassy one every time, because they know they can strike the ball cleanly and really control the shot. Once you learn to use the same aggressive swing technique, you'll conquer tight lies, too.

Stay loose; keep your arms relaxed and your body in motion to encourage an active, lively swing. Address the ball about one ball width back from the standard left heel position, and put 70 percent of your weight on your left side. This ensures that you'll contact the ball first with the clubhead descending.

Your body will dominate the swinging action, while the arms follow and the hands remain quiet. Swing back fully so your weight shifts to the inside of the right leg. The key to a successful shot is a strong weight shift onto the left foot to start the downswing, with the left hip clearing and the left hand, arm, and shoulder pulling the club down into the back of the ball.

Trust the loft of the clubface to get the ball up despite the descending blow you've delivered. The good news is that since your strong impact position has effectively decreased the club's natural loft, you can play the shot with a 6-iron from where you'd normally need a 5, and still put the shot pin high.

Shot Eight—Lofted Wood from Deep Rough

I believe all amateurs except perhaps scratch players should always carry a 5-wood or even a 6-wood in their bags. These "utility" clubs make approaches in the 170- to 200-yard range from medium or deep rough seem like a breeze, as compared to muscling the ball with a long iron.

In this situation, you want to swing the lofted wood as if it were a middle iron. Assume an open stance with your feet a little closer together than normal, slightly less than shoulder width apart. This type of stance promotes a narrower, more up-and-down swing arc than for a standard fairway wood shot. Your hands should be ahead of the ball slightly with your weight favoring the left side more than normal.

Be sure to rotate, or "clear" your left hip to the left on the downswing, when hitting off a tight lie.

Make sure to raise or hover the clubhead just above the deep grass at address, to ensure that you don't snag it in the rough going back. Your arms should dominate the backswing motion while your head remains steady and less weight shifts to your right side than normal. Then pull the club down, holding on firmly with the left hand.

The shallow face of the lofted wood plus its broad sole (which spreads the grass around at impact) make this shot easier to hit than with a long iron. You can get plenty of height on the shot, and since it should fade just a touch with proper execution, it will sit down quickly, too, upon landing.

Shot Nine— The Flyer

When your ball comes to rest in light rough, the shot looks much simpler than one from the thick "spinach." However, it can be tricky, particularly when the grass blades are lying in the direction of the hole. Often the ball will fly off the clubface hot, like it was shot out of a cannon, and run a long way upon landing, too. What you have is a flyer lie.

There are two adjustments you can make to counteract some of this flyer effect:

1. Play the ball back slightly in your stance; this will allow less grass to intervene between the clubface and the ball at impact.
2. Choke down on the grip to keep your swing arc fairly narrow.

Even with these precautions, the ball will come out pretty hot. So always take a more lofted club than you would from the same distance with a good fairway lie, and remember to make a one-piece follow-through.

Shot Ten—Hook Around Trees

Golf galleries are always amazed at the pros' ability to play their way out of trouble by bending the ball sharply around obstacles. However, assuming you have a reasonable lie, playing a sweeping hook when your path is blocked by trees is not as difficult as it looks.

On wood shots from deep rough, raise the club above the grass— "hover" it—when you assume your address position.

In playing a shot from a flyer lie, *choke down* on the club a little more to promote an upright swing plane.

First, align your clubface to the spot you want the ball to finish. In all likelihood, this will mean the clubface is actually aiming directly at the tree or other obstacle you're trying to avoid. While this may sound a bit scary, remember that the ball will start out along the path of your swing, not the clubface angle. So carefully align your body to the right of the obstacle, so the starting line of the ball's flight will also be to the right of the target.

When gripping, you should see between three and four knuckles on your left hand, meaning the grip is much stronger than normal.

Stand a little farther from the ball than you ordinarily would, to encourage a flatter, more inside-out swing path. Since the clubface will be closed in relation to the target line, it will also carry less loft than normal. Thus a 4-iron will play like a 2 and a 7-iron more like a 5.

Help yourself stay loose over the ball by waggling the club actively, away and then back to the ball a few times. This will help program an extra-free swinging action in the hit zone, encouraging the toe of the club to pass the heel. The shot will start out low and right of the tree, then turn sharply left. It will stay low and pitch with plenty of overspin, so plan to land the ball well short and let it run onto the green.

Practice this shot, for the low hook is a great weapon, particularly in match play when you want to shake up an opponent.

Shot Eleven— Slice Around Trees

The sister to the hook shot is the long slice, to bend the ball right around trees that obscure your route to the green.

Basically, your setup tactics for this shot are the opposite of those just described for the low hook. While your clubface points to where you want the ball to finish, align your feet, knees, hips, and shoulders well left of the tree or other obstacle that blocks your path to the green.

Your grip should be weak, with only one knuckle showing; this hold helps keep the clubface open in relation to your swing path.

Stand a little closer to the ball than normal, so your swing arc automatically becomes more upright. Swing the club along your

When you need to hit a severe hook around trees, assume an extra *strong* grip.

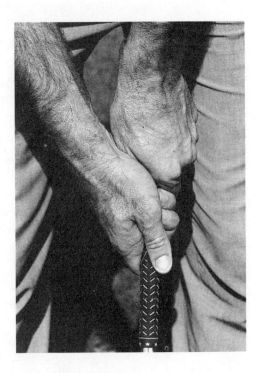

body line while holding on firmly with your left hand, to make sure the clubface stays open through impact. The ball will curve right in a long crescent and land fairly softly, so plan to carry the ball almost all the way to your target.

Keep in mind that since the clubface is open in relation to your swing path, it will carry extra loft at impact. So always take one or two clubs stronger for the intentional slice than you would from the same distance in the fairway.

Shot Twelve—Under a Branch

Often you'll find yourself so close to a tree that it's impossible to play a hook or slice around it. If you have a relatively clean lie, though, maybe you can hit the ball under the branches.

The most important point here is to pick the club that you know can keep the ball beneath the limbs. Here's a tip to help you determine that club: Step to the side of the ball and the tree and

Aiming your body well left of target and holding on to the club more firmly with your *left* hand, when coming into the ball, will allow you to hit a controlled slice.

visualize the starting trajectory of the shot. Often you'll get a much more accurate appraisal from the side than you can from behind the ball. Also, always plan to keep the ball under the lowest branch by at least a couple of feet as an insurance policy.

Correct club in hand, address the shot with the ball centered in your stance, hands ahead of the clubface and 75 percent of your weight on your left side. Make a three-quarter backswing; then hit sharply through the ball. The ball will start very low, staying under the tree limbs; then the backspin will take effect, causing the ball to rise later in its flight.

One word of warning: Never try to force a low shot under branches from heavy rough. The odds are that in trying to dig the ball up out of the rough, you'll hit the branches.

Shot Thirteen— Over the Tree

When you find yourself behind a tree you can't get under or curve the ball around, consider the over-the-tree option. But before deciding to go for it, make sure there's enough cushion under the ball so you can fully utilize the club's loft and get the shot up quickly. Also, make sure this gamble is worth it, meaning that you can get the ball over the tree and still reach the green.

Assuming the lie is very good and you're confident that you can hit the shot home, again stand to the side and visualize the trajectory you need to clear the treetop. Once you've selected a club, play the ball slightly forward in your stance, opposite your left instep, with your head and upper body behind the ball and your weight favoring your right side. Keep your grip pressure very light to encourage a full, free-swinging action. Concentrate on making a complete hip and shoulder turnaway from the ball while swinging the arms back on an upright plane. Your downswing key is to keep the head steady and behind the ball. The club's lowest point will be just behind the ball, so you will contact it slightly on the upswing. Strive for a full, upright finish, letting your head swivel up as you follow through.

To hit an approach shot under branches, make a *three-quarter* backswing, then hit sharply *through* the ball.

Concentrating on finishing *high* will help you hit a high shot.

**Shot Fourteen—
Off Hardpan**

Once off the manicured fairways, firm dirt areas, or hardpan, often come into play. Most handicap players try to pick the ball cleanly off hardpan, with the most common result being a topped shot. Try this aggressive approach and your results will quickly improve.

Select one club stronger than you would for the same shot from the fairway. Choke down slightly for control and play the ball pretty much in the middle of your stance. Your stance line and your shoulders should point a few yards left of the target while the clubface remains square. Swing normally, emphasizing a strong weight shift onto the left side on the downswing so that the clubhead follows, delivering a sharp descending blow.

Make sure to keep your right wrist flexed back so there's no flippiness of the clubhead through the impact zone. Because of the sharper-than-normal downswing angle, you should finish with the hands low and the clubshaft pointing to the target. The ball will start low, then rise to its apex while drifting slightly right. It will "bite" the green with plenty of spin, so plan on carrying the ball almost all the way to the hole.

**Shot Fifteen—
The Skip Shot**

The match is on the line and you're confronted by a water hazard guarding the green. Worse yet, tree branches block your line in such a way that you can't play under them and fly the ball over the water, and you're too close to them to play over them.

Instead of chipping out sideways so you still face a tough third, play the skip shot instead.

The key to this daring, yet effective shot is to apply right-to-left spin to the ball, which keeps it low and makes it dart forward across the water's surface. Depending on the lie and the length of shot, select a middle to long iron. Align your body to the right of the pin, while hooding the clubface so it points toward the target. Keep your weight on your left side and grip lightly.

Because a low right-to-left flight is imperative, the hands and forearms should be more active in this swing. Turn them clockwise early in the backswing, then counterclockwise through the impact zone so that the toe of the club is moving from an open to a closed

In setting up to hit a shot off hardpan, set the clubface down *squarely* behind the ball.

position. The finish should be low with the right hand on top of the club.

Aim for a spot within 20 yards of the far edge of the water hazard. The ball will skip either once or twice on the water before scooting up the bank and onto the green—to the dismay of your opponent!

Shot Sixteen— Wood from Fairway Bunker

When you've driven into a fairway bunker on a long par four, chances are you're reconciled to playing your second shot well short of the green. However, if the lie is good and there's little or no lip on the trap, why not try for the green with a lofted fairway wood?

Strive for a *low* finish when playing the skip shot.

In setting up to play this bold shot successfully, work your feet securely into the sand until you can feel your spikes reaching the sand's base. Your stance should be wider than normal, slightly wider than your shoulders, to promote a wide-bottomed swing arc.

Grip down on the club you've selected in order to compensate for the fact that digging in has brought you slightly closer to the ball. Make sure to hover the club above the sand's surface because any contact with the sand means you'll incur a penalty stroke.

Strive to make a slow, relatively low takeaway, with your arms swinging the club back. Swing up to a compact three-quarter position to ensure all-important good balance. Turn your left hip to the left to lead the downswing, and maintain the pressure on your right

When playing a wood shot from a fairway bunker, it's important that you take a *wide* stance and make a compact backswing.

knee. Try to meet the back of the ball as levelly as possible and swing your arms through to a full finish. You should get all but about five yards of your normal lofted-wood distance from the fairway.

Shot Seventeen— Lefty Recovery

Every so often, a tee shot will come to rest so close to a tree or bush that there's no way to address the ball normally to play a right-handed shot. Instead of declaring the lie unplayable and accepting a penalty stroke, with a little practice you can learn to advance the ball nicely by hitting it left-handed.

You'll hit the shot with the face of an iron club turned upside down. Because you want a fair amount of hitting surface but not too much loft, I believe a 5-iron is a good choice.

Make the lefty recovery a compact arm swing, with no substantial weight shift. Your main swing thought should be to keep the head very still and avoid lurching through the shot in your anxiety to see the results. Try to watch the upside-down clubface meet the ball. Remember, the ball will go a little to the right of your swing path because of the loft on the upside-down clubface.

You may feel extremely awkward on your first few attempts, which is why I'd like to see these swings take place during practice. You'll find, however, that with repetition, clean contact and distance will come. You may be able to make left-handed recoveries of up to 100 yards—and save a stroke in the process.

When stymied by a tree, turn a 5-iron *upside down* and hit a left-handed recovery shot.

**RITSON'S
REVIEW**

Here is a summary of the seventeen "big shots," with a key thought for each:

- *Shot One*—From a Divot: Use extra loft and hit down sharply.
- *Shot Two*—Cuppy Lie: Employ an outside-in swing path.
- *Shot Three*—Downhill Lie: Swing down the slope.
- *Shot Four*—Uphill Lie: Swing up the slope.
- *Shot Five*—Ball Above Feet: Choke down on the club more than normal.
- *Shot Six*—Ball Below Feet: Keep your weight on your heels.
- *Shot Seven*—Tight Lie: Position the ball back in your stance.
- *Shot Eight*—Lofted Wood from Deep Rough: Employ a steep swing arc.
- *Shot Nine*—The Flyer: Take a more lofted club.
- *Shot Ten*—Hook Around Trees: Strengthen your grip.
- *Shot Eleven*—Slice Around Trees: Aim your body well left of the tree.
- *Shot Twelve*—Under a Branch: Pick the right club to keep the ball low.
- *Shot Thirteen*—Over the Tree: Stay behind the ball.
- *Shot Fourteen*—Off Hardpan: Make a strong weight shift on the downswing.
- *Shot Fifteen*—The Skip Shot: Rotate your hands and arms more vigorously during the swing.
- *Shot Sixteen*—Wood from Fairway Bunker: Assume a wide stance.
- *Shot Seventeen*—Lefty Recovery: Practice "opposite" swing feel.

8 GOING STRAIGHT

These cures for a faulty swing will help you straighten out your crooked shots

It's a terrific sensation to step onto the first tee for a weekend round of golf, feeling complete faith in your ability to hit straight, solid shots. The fine amateur player possesses that confidence; he knows his swing will work essentially on automatic pilot and that his shotmaking prowess will allow him to deal with the demands of tough situations off the fairway if he does happen to get a bad bounce or make a strategic error.

Unfortunately, the vast majority of amateur players never attain this level of confidence or competence in their swings. The truth of the matter is, they hit many more crooked, popped-up, or topped shots per round than they do straight ones. This fact is borne out by the scores that amateurs report that they shoot, which show that the average golfer in this country scores about 99. Since most courses play to a par of 72, this means that Mr. Average is about 27 strokes over par per round!

Let's assume this average golfer is taking an average of 36 putts per round, which converts to a par round on the greens. This means the player is shooting approximately 27 over par per round on the shots from tee to green alone. That is an awful lot of poor swings in 18 holes. Sadly, I believe many club-level players expect to mishit the majority of their shots. They seem to be happy if, during the course of 18 holes, they play 2 or 3 of them precisely by the book. Even if they double-bogey all the rest, those few good holes are enough to bring them back.

Well, I applaud the love for the game that these long-suffering middle- and high-handicappers exhibit. But at the same time, their level of play truly upsets me because in most cases I am certain they could do much better. Frankly, if they would just learn to hit shots a little better, they would surely enjoy the game all the more. I ask you: Instead of hitting just a couple of fairways and two or three greens in regulation per round, how would you like to hit, say, ten of your eighteen tee shots in the fairway, and ten greens in regulation, with several legitimate birdie putts per round? I'm here to tell you that it's not impossible.

In order to accomplish a much higher standard of ball striking, however, you must eliminate the major swing faults that are sabotaging your tee-to-green game. It's hard to explain why so many amateurs have developed the wide variety of swing faults that I see every day on the practice tee. Perhaps they've never had the benefit of professional instruction and are not aware of what's causing their problems. Or they *think* they are employing the proper swing movements that their golf professionals taught them, but somewhere along the line they got lost.

In this chapter, I describe what I truly believe are the most damaging swing faults in golf. Then I explain in detail how you can rid yourself once and for all of these unwanted bad moves. You may already know which of these flaws is plaguing your game. Or, by reading this chapter and comparing the faults described with the moves you make in your own swing, you may very well identify faults you didn't know you had. Either way, the information that follows will help your game immensely.

The Flying Right Elbow

You develop maximum power on the backswing by making as complete a turn of the hips and shoulders away from the target as possible. The swing of the arms should remain connected to this turn of the torso so that the swing remains under control and stays on a consistent plane. However, many amateurs, in a vain attempt to put more power into their shots, go to the wrong source. Instead of increasing their body turn, they lift the club with their arms near the completion of the backswing. The right elbow thus flies away from the body, pointing toward the sky rather than down at the

A *levering* action of the right forearm will help you keep your right elbow in fairly close to your side on the backswing.

ground. This faulty flying right elbow position usually forces the clubshaft to point across the target line at the top of the backswing. Consequently, a player who has this fault finds it very difficult to bring the club back down on the correct inside-to-along-the-line path. The result: inconsistent shots that fly either far left or far right of the target.

Cure: Change your mental emphasis regarding what really swings the golf club. It is your body coil on the backswing, and its uncoiling on the downswing, that produces a wide swing arc and powerful shots. You should never attempt to lift the club independently with both arms on the backswing. Instead, as you turn your right hip and shoulder away from the ball, simply lever your right forearm up from the elbow. This levering action will pull your left arm up onto the proper backswing plane and keep your right elbow pointing down in the process. Most important, your arms will no longer outrun your body's backswing turn and disrupt the swing plane.

When you make this right forearm levering motion rather than lifting your arms, your swing will acquire a feeling of tightness that it lacked before. Your swing plane will become much more consistent and you will virtually automatically deliver the club squarely to the ball.

The Severely Bent Left Elbow

Another way many amateurs lose control on the backswing is to bend the left elbow severely at the top of the swing.

This fault is usually traced to a bad setup; the player puts too much weight on his left foot and sets his hands too far ahead of the ball. Both of these faults cause him to swing back on a steep angle (with a "broken" left arm), release his hands too early ("cast" them) on the downswing, and hit a weak slice shot.

To cure the "broken" left arm problem, set up so your left arm, left hand, and the clubshaft form an *unbroken* line.

Cure: Balance your weight evenly: 50 percent on the ball of each foot. Also, line your hands up with the ball.

Since the setup largely determines the type of motion you make, these two subtle changes will allow you to swing the club back smoothly on a shallower angle. Therefore, the left arm will maintain its radius, the release action will be better, and your shots will fly straighter.

Tailoring the tip: *Remember that the left arm needn't be tense and ramrod straight—an ever so slight bend or "softness" at the elbow will allow you to maintain a fluid swinging motion.*

Swaying Off the Ball

Another major error the typical high-handicap player makes is to severely rock or sway his upper body away from the target on the backswing. This exaggerated lateral movement is usually an honest effort by the golfer to get his weight properly onto the right side on the backswing, so he or she can return the weight to the left side on the downswing and hit with power. However, swaying the upper body to the right is a deadly error because it's almost impossible to rock back to exactly the same position from which you started. Pushed and pulled shots are the most common results.

Cure: Make a point of keeping your head rock steady, so you get the feeling that you are waiting for your left shoulder to turn under your chin.

Now you'll make a good upper body coil on the backswing and naturally shift your weight onto a firmly flexed right knee, instead of allowing your right side to sway to the right. Consequently, you'll be readied to unwind powerfully and hit a strong, straight shot.

If you have a problem swaying off the ball on the backswing, concentrate on keeping your head *still* and turning your left shoulder under your *chin*.

The Reverse Pivot

The reverse pivot is basically the opposite flaw of the sway to the right. Instead of shifting the weight onto the right knee and right heel as the backswing progresses, the player leaves all of the weight that was on his or her left side at address in place, or even increases the amount of weight on the left foot. The only weight shift that *can* occur on the downswing, then, is a falling-away move to the right. With this reverse weight shift, a fat shot will usually result and a topped shot is the next unhappy alternative.

Cure: Make an aggressive rotary hip turn on the backswing. In slow motion, turn your right hip around to the right as fully as possible. As you do this, notice how your weight automatically shifts onto your right heel. Now you have fully loaded your weight onto your right side and are poised to make a powerful weight shift to the left on the downswing.

Practice this rotary hip turn around your right knee frequently and your reverse weight shift will become a thing of the past.

If your number one swing fault is a reverse pivot, encourage a good weight shift on the backswing by turning your *right hip*.

Overly Flat Swing Plane

The correct plane along which the golf club moves during the swing will vary somewhat from player to player. The tall golfer should exhibit a fairly upright arc, while the short player's swing will revolve on a slightly flatter or more horizontal plane.

Regardless of individual height, some amateurs swing on too flat a plane relative to their physical stature. This overly flat backswing prevents the golfer from returning the club to a straight position at impact. Unless the ball is positioned just perfectly in the stance, either a pushed or a pulled shot results. Also, since the clubhead is delivered on such a shallow path, the flat swing plane proves very ineffective in hitting from the rough.

One sure remedy for a flat swing is to practice hitting shots from a severe *open* stance.

Cure: You're currently whipping your hands and your arms too much around your body. To remedy this fault, hit practice shots from an open stance, with your left foot pulled back considerably from the target line. You'll find that your hands *must* move more vertically than around on the backswing in order to avoid hitting your right leg.

Gradually, this practice tip will ingrain the feel of a more upright arm swing into your motion on the course. Therefore, you'll likely return the clubface smack into the back of the ball at impact and hit powerfully accurate shots from the fairway or rough.

**Swing Too
Upright**

I believe that, if anything, more club players swing on a plane that's too upright rather than too flat, meaning that they angle the club straight up on the backswing rather than behind them. Therefore, while the clubhead will move through the impact zone more along the target line, it will also be moving on too steep an angle for solid contact to be made with the ball. If the ball's a little too far back in the stance, you'll top the shot, or if it's too far forward, you'll hit it fat, or heavy. Furthermore, however, even with the perfect ball position, the too-upright swing can cause you to hit tee shots with too much backspin, causing the ball to upshoot so that you lose distance.

Cure: Strengthen your grip (so you see two and one-half knuckles of your left hand when you look down) and play the ball off the heel of the club. Both of these address keys will automatically promote a less upright swing. Consequently, you'll hit the ball more like a pro than an amateur.

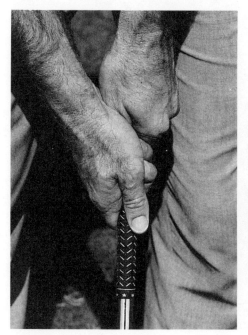

Assuming a *two-and-one-half* knuckle grip (photo–left) and addressing the ball off the *heel* of the clubface (photo–below) will cure your faulty, upright plane problem.

Dipping the Right Shoulder

Fat shots abound when the golfer drastically lowers his or her right shoulder when bringing the club into the impact zone. Undoubtedly this move occurs when the player seeks to apply some extra power to the shot. However, not only does the right-shoulder dip throw the clubhead into the ground before it contacts the ball, but it's a faulty method of supplying power to the shot to begin with.

Cure: Power is transmitted to the clubhead (via the arms, then the hands, then the clubshaft) most efficiently through the buildup of centrifugal force, which is a pulling rather than a pushing motion. Therefore, the best way to stop dipping your right shoulder is to simply ignore it as a conscious source of power. Instead, once you start your downswing with a distinct pulling action of your left hip and side, consciously whip your hands, arms, and the club into the ball.

Concentrating on swinging the club through with your *hands* and *arms* will cure your "shoulder dip" problem.

The Lower Body Lunge

Some golfers make a good attempt to shift their weight onto the left side at the start of the downswing. Unfortunately, this well-intended shift often becomes more of a lunge with the legs, causing the upper body to follow. Since the head and upper body must stay behind the ball on the downswing, this fault prevents the clubface from returning to a square position at impact. It arrives in an open position, with the result being a wayward push shot to the right of target.

To prevent a lower-body lunge on the downswing, rotate your left knee, left hip, and left pants pocket to your *left*.

Cure: To stop the lunge, make what I refer to as a "turn-away" action on the downswing. Rather than shifting your lower body laterally in a violent fashion—lunging—simultaneously rotate your left knee, left hip, and left pants pocket to your left and rear the second your hands drop to thigh level.

You will then be able to square up the clubface without any artificial manipulation, and find yourself suddenly hitting the ball much straighter.

Outside-In Swing Plane

Cutting across the ball on the downswing is yet another common fault of all middle- to high-handicap players. On short iron shots, this downswing fault causes the ball to fly left of the target. On shots with clubs that feature a lesser degree of loft, the ball will start left and move quickly right of target. The outside-in swing path that causes you to cut across the ball is the result of an attempt to hit *at* the ball with the right arm and shoulder.

Cure: Although I would never teach you to drop your right elbow straight down against your right side at the start of the downswing, in this case I will, to cure your problem. You do not have to swing your arms out at the ball, because the turning of your hips and torso will automatically bring your arms and hands out and around and allow the club to meet the ball squarely. Drop your elbow against your side so that your hands remain directly behind you as you start down. Trust your body turn to swing your arms, hands, and the clubface into the ball from the inside to along the target line, and you'll be extremely pleased with the results.

The best way to solve an outside-in swing plane problem is to drop your *right elbow* against your side on the downswing.

Inside-Out Swing Plane

A swing plane that delivers the club from too far inside the target line will usually cause you to hit a big hook. This overly inside swing plane is somewhat less common than the severe outside-in plane previously described. More often than not, its cause is incorrect alignment at address in which the body is closed to the target line, aiming right of target.

Cure: Square up your address position. To help you square up to your target—feet, knees, hips, and shoulders parallel to the target line—have a friend lay a club along your toes as you address the ball. Then step back and look; if the club is not parallel to an imaginary line running from the ball to the target, return to your address position until you work yourself into a square setup; your friend will confirm that. If, after making the correction, you notice that your shots are still starting a little right of the target, move the ball up in your stance. This adjustment should assure that you contact the ball right at the point where the clubhead is moving along the target line.

In curing an inside-out
swing plane problem,
stand behind the ball
to check that the club
across your toes is
parallel, or "square,"
to the target line.

Standing Up on the Shot

Many golfers rarely experience the feeling of striking the golf ball truly flush with the middle, or "sweet spot," of the clubface. The reason is: The typical high handicapper stands up through the impact zone, straightening his legs, with the result usually being a topped shot that runs along the ground.

Most golfers think they lift their heads in these instances. Usually, however, the head itself is not the culprit. Again, the cause is standing up or losing the flex in the knees during the downswing.

Cure: Shift your weight to the outside of your left foot. (You'll know you're doing this if you look down and see that the toes of your left foot are off the ground.)

This one key will allow you to stay down through impact and, in turn, enable you to hit more powerfully through the ball.

Whether you're hitting an iron or a wood, shifting your weight onto your *left foot* will allow you to retain your knee flex on the downswing.

The Reverse C

The Reverse C is a phrase used by golfers to describe a faulty follow-through in which the body finishes with the hips thrust well forward and the back arched to the maximum. The body, in silhouette, looks like a big reversed C. This follow-through indicates an overly aggressive move through the ball. The exaggerated degree of downswing body movement that creates the Reverse C means controlling the direction of your shots will be quite difficult; and the Reverse C finish puts a tremendous strain on your back to boot, which can easily lead to strain or injury.

Cure: Instead of driving the left hip and side directly at your target, make your downswing hip turn in more of a rotary movement. By turning your left hip in a counterclockwise direction (around to your left rear), your entire torso will also be turning in rotary fashion through the shot. This turning action not only aids greatly in helping you deliver the clubface square to the ball, it pulls you into a follow-through in which your body finishes in a more erect position, facing the target. It's a true swinging rather than a heaving action that will certainly add several more accurate and pain-free years to your golfing life.

Turning your left hip in
a counterclockwise
direction on the
downswing will cure
your "reverse C"
problem.

Wrong Release

Many high-handicap golfers make a perfect backswing but then mess up the downswing. The typical player rotates his right forearm-hand unit so vigorously in a counterclockwise direction that the clubface closes at impact, causing the ball to "duck hook"— fly left off the clubface, then dart farther left in the air. This shot rolls more, too, which makes matters worse when the ball is headed for trouble to begin with.

Cure: The best way to remedy this swing fault is to stand in a sand trap and hit blast shots. Purposely hit down into a spot about two inches behind the ball. Trying to hit down encourages you to work your right forearm under your left, rather than dramatically over it.

This technique is particularly critical on short-iron and medium-iron shots to the green, when you must hit down sharply to impart maximum backspin on the ball.

Practicing sand shots will help you work your right forearm *under* your left.

**RITSON'S
REVIEW**

Here are the swing keys to keep foremost in mind to cure the most common swing faults:

- Flying Right Elbow: Keep your upper right arm relatively close to your side on the backswing.
- Bent Left Elbow: Align your hands even with the ball at address.
- Swaying off the Ball: Keep your head rock steady.
- Reverse Pivot: Turn your right hip in a clockwise direction on the backswing.
- Overly Flat Swing Plane: Hit shots from an open stance.
- Swing Too Upright: Strengthen your grip.
- Dipping Right Shoulder: Whip the club through the ball with your hands and arms.
- Lower Body Lunge: Rotate your left knee to your left.
- Outside-In Swing Plane: Drop your right elbow against your side on the downswing.
- Inside-Out Swing Plane: Square up your address.
- Standing Up on the Shot: Shift your weight to the outside of your left foot.
- Reverse C: Make a rotary hip turn.
- Wrong Release: Keep your right forearm under your left.

9 | DRILL TIME

These drills will help you practice with a purpose and play better golf

Up to this point, you have assimilated a wealth of knowledge that can't help but make you an improved golfer. Of course, there's a difference between reading this material and grasping it on an intellectual basis, and physically putting the advice to good use on the course. That's where practice comes in.

Naturally, the more you wish to improve, the more you will need to practice all aspects of your game. But please keep in mind that it is the *quality* of your practice that is crucial. The *quantity* of your practice, whether you count it in hours or in numbers of balls hit, will only help you in relation to the quality of thought and the precision that go into your sessions.

If you are a member of a golf club with a reasonably large membership, you probably know several golfers who really seem to work hard at their games. You'll see them on the practice tee before and after their weekend rounds, and they show up after work a couple of evenings a week, too. They hit thousands of practice balls every year and put in lots of time around the practice green. This dedication is truly admirable, but there's one problem: They never get any better, and sometimes they get worse.

Why does this happen to so many dedicated golfers? They don't adhere to an organized plan when they practice. They don't break down the fundamental principles of the setup and swing. They don't simplify their sessions by paying attention to just one setup or swing item at a time. Instead, they try to improve on everything at once. They resort to grab-bag tips from anyone who has a so-called great idea. Furthermore, they believe that simply hitting balls is a guarantee of improvement. If this were true, then the people who hit the most balls would always be the best players. Obviously, this is not the case.

So you must learn to hit every practice shot with a purpose. And you must stick religiously with the correct swing movements outlined here.

I realize that it's quite easy to stray from your swing principles during practice, so in this chapter, I will provide you with twenty-five drills or reminders to help keep you focused and practicing with a purpose. These drills cover a variety of areas, from how to groove the correct address position to how to sink a pressure putt; many do not even require you to hit shots, so you can work on them at home as well as on the practice tee.

Drill One—Clap for Good Posture

Here's a step-by-step procedure for attaining a super address posture on full shots:

1. Stand with your feet shoulder-width apart with your arms at your sides.
2. Bring your hands out in front of you and clap them together at thigh height.
3. While keeping your arms and hands in this clap position, bend from the waist so that your spine is lowered at about a 25-degree angle.
4. Slide or shift your left hip slightly toward the target. You'll notice that as you do this, your right hip, shoulder, and arm

The Good Posture Drill: Step One

The Good Posture Drill: Step Two

The Good Posture Drill: Step Three

The Good Posture Drill: Step Four

automatically lower slightly, so that your right hand is also lowered a couple of inches below your left, just as it will be when you grip the club.

This clap drill puts you in an excellent address position. Your left side is dominant. Your right side is in a soft, slightly lowered position, and your head is behind the ball.

Drill Two—The "Non-Milkman" Grip

Most right-handed amateurs unconsciously turn their left hands too far to the right, toward too strong a position. I refer to this as "milking" the grip. Here's how to prevent it: Start assuming your left-hand grip from *underneath* the handle, exerting pressure with your last three fingers of that hand from underneath the grip. Then close your palm, thumb, and forefinger lightly over the club's handle.

I find that golfers who start by putting pressure on the top of the grip, rather than underneath, invariably wind up with the palm too far on top of the handle. Keep the pressure on from underneath with the last three fingers and the palm will close naturally into the correct position with two knuckles showing.

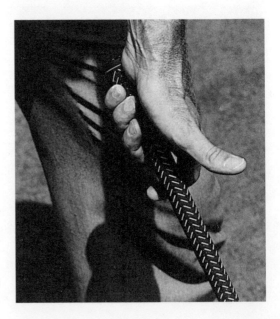

Discourage "milking" by gripping firmly with the last three fingers of your left hand.

**Drill Three—
One-Armed
Swing**

Your left arm should be extended, but not stiff, at the address position. This arm should also be virtually fully extended but not stiff at the top of the swing as well.

Here's a way to ingrain the proper feel for this left arm position: Grip the club at address with your left hand only, while placing your right arm behind your back. Practice swinging to the top of the backswing with your left arm only. You won't be able to swing back until your left shoulder muscles become fairly taut.

With your right hand off the club, it can't force your left arm to bend into an overswinging position, which is a common flaw among club-level golfers. Likewise, it can't push the left arm out into an extra-stiff position which hampers a rhythmic swing.

The one-arm drill will give you a good *feel* for the correct left arm position on the backswing.

**Drill Four—
Rotate Around
Your Right Knee**

In order to make a solid backswing, your body must stay centered while still turning and coiling to develop power. The trick is to move your weight onto your right side while the right knee maintains its original slightly flexed, soft position. Two common faults are to lock the right knee on the backswing, or to allow the right knee to sway to the right as it accepts the weight.

In this exercise, make a slower-than-normal backswing, but instead of watching the ball, observe your right knee's position. By watching the knee, you almost guarantee you will keep it in its original position, even if you normally buckle or lock it. Keep making practice backswings while watching your right knee, and very soon this steady weight-bearing position will become second nature.

Keep your right knee flex position in check by *watching* it while you swing.

**Drill Five—Left
Knee Behind the
Ball**

This practice technique builds on the previous exercise. On the driver backswing, you must be sure to get your body weight into your right side. To make a good weight transfer, focus on your left knee movement laterally to the right.

Once again, make slow backswings with your driver, this time watching your left knee instead of your right. While you are still maintaining a stable right knee position, your left knee should move laterally to the right, behind the ball.

Keep a check on your left knee position by *watching* it while you swing.

Drill Six—Put Weight on Your Right Heel

Most golfers either slice or pull their shots because of a severe out-to-in path. Shifting your weight onto the outside or the toes of the right foot on the backswing almost guarantees this faulty swing path.

To counteract this tendency, practice your backswing and feel your weight moving onto the *heel* of your right foot.

Practice shifting your weight onto the *heel* of your right foot to stop mishit, off-line shots.

**Drill Seven—
Wind It Up!**

Every golfer must strive to wind up the large muscles of the hips, torso, and shoulders to the maximum. Many golfers have the impression they've wound up because they get the club back a long way, but they've really done it by collapsing the left arm and both wrists.

Here's a good turn-building technique. Stand up to the ball with a club hooked behind your lower back at the elbows (the butt end should be behind your left side). Make slow backswing turns, controlling your weight shift with your right knee steady, while your left knee moves behind the ball as described. Try to continue turning until the butt end of the club points well behind (to the right of) the ball. When you can accomplish this while maintaining balance, you've made a good, athletic turn.

Here's the best exercise for learning how to make an *athletic* turn.

**Drill Eight—
Correcting Your
Backswing Foot
Fault**

Here is a proven tip for correcting the most common right foot fault—moving the weight onto the outside of the right foot during the backswing, which leads to spinning out on the downswing.

To cure this fault, place a middle iron on the ground behind your right foot, with its clubhead wedged under that foot. Then swing a few times. You'll soon feel how the wedge promotes the proper weight shift.

Practicing your swing with a club *wedged* under your right foot will stop you from swaying on the backswing and spinning out on the downswing.

Drill Nine—The Waiter's Drill

You've probably heard advice to keep your elbow from flying away from your body at the top of the backswing. However, tucking the elbow completely down and against the side is also counterproductive because it overly restricts the swing arc and reduces power.

Here's how to establish the optimum elbow position: Practice swinging your right arm back without a club (keep the left arm behind your back). At the top of the backswing, your right hand should be positioned as if you were a waiter carrying a tray. When in this position, your elbow will be pointing down nicely, yet remaining freely away from your body.

Holding an imaginary *tray* at the top of your swing will train you to employ the correct right elbow position.

Drill Ten—Check for Elbow No-No

Here's another simple double-check to see that you're not keeping your right elbow too tight to the body, which creates a very narrow swing arc and a faulty clubshaft position at the top of the backswing.

Place a golf ball under your right armpit. When you swing up to the top, the ball should drop out. If it doesn't, you know your elbow's in too tight (and your "waiter's tray" has tipped over, too)!

When you swing, the ball you put under your right armpit better *fall* out, otherwise your right elbow is tucked in too close to your body.

**Drill Eleven—
Consistent Grip
Pressure—For
Just 25 Cents!**

Many players tend to lose control of the club, particularly when they complete their backswing.

The best way to maintain a steady hold of the club at the top is to squeeze the lifeline of your right palm upward against your left thumb.

Here's a great way to check on this subtle but important point:

1. Place a quarter on top of your left thumb;
2. Close your right palm over your left thumb, as normally;
3. Swing the club to the top; stop; then look at your hands.

If the quarter stayed in place, you maintained good, steady "lifeline pressure." If not, keep practicing this "squeeze play."

Twenty-Five Cent Lesson: Step One

Twenty-Five Cent Lesson: Step Two

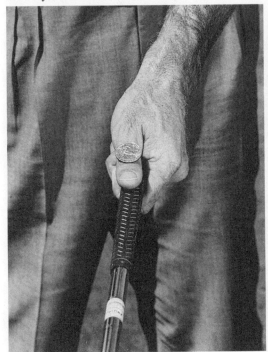

Twenty-Five Cent Lesson: Step Three

Drill Twelve—Go Bowlegged Starting Down

The optimum downswing features a strong initiating move by the lower left side, building up centrifugal force to be released by the right side at impact. A useful key is to start the downswing by moving the left knee down the toe line, so that the distance between your knees is momentarily increased. At this point you should then look a little *bowlegged* and in a sitting position with both knees flexed.

Practice this left knee move to the target and the "sitting down" position in front of a mirror at home. Then blend it into your swing on the practice tee.

Going *bowlegged* in practice can help you in play.

**Drill Thirteen—
Get "Hip" for
Downswing
Power**

Immediately after the left knee has moved down the line of your feet to start the downswing, you should clear your left hip to the left and rear (in counterclockwise fashion) to develop power and give your arms room for a clear swing through impact.

To coach yourself on this move, address the ball with your left hand on the club while your right hand rests on your right hip. Swing up to the top. Then, after you've shifted your left knee, use your right hand to literally *push* your hip through the impact zone. The impetus from your right hand and right hip will force your left hip to freely clear. Soon you'll have the feel of this hip clearance in your normal swing, without any prompting from your right hand.

Push your hip through to acquaint yourself with the proper downswing "clearing" movement.

**Drill Fourteen—
Be Underhanded**

Coming over the top with the upper right side, forcing the clubhead outside the target line, is a common downswing flaw. Here's a drill to help you ingrain the feeling of correct right-side movement.

Assume your address, and then imagine that you are tossing a ball underhanded toward your target.

Next, swing and physically repeat the underhanded motion, using the club rather than your hand to do the tossing on the downswing.

This underhanded tossing sensation keeps the clubhead approaching the ball correctly from inside to along the target line.

Imagining yourself *tossing* a ball underhanded will help you swing through correctly.

**Drill Fifteen—
Chase with the
Right Knee**

Only when you have started the downswing correctly with the left knee and then the left hip can you release the power of your right side through the ball. At this point, halfway through the downswing, strive to make your right knee narrow the distance between it and your left knee (which you increased at the very start of the downswing). By making your right knee *chase* your left, you move virtually all your weight onto your left side through impact. You are also fully utilizing your lower body in the downswing before the right hand, arm, and shoulder release the club at impact.

Make your right knee *chase* your left knee on the downswing to promote a full release of the right side.

**Drill Sixteen—
Freeze the
Perfect Follow-
Through**

From midway through the downswing to midway through the follow-through, your left arm should rotate completely. That is, halfway down, the *outside* of the left forearm should face away from you; halfway through the follow-through, the *inside* of your forearm should face away from you. This complete rotation of the forearm also means the clubface has rotated fully in the hit zone.

To aid this release, use the following drill: Make practice swings with your left arm only (right arm behind your back). Swing your left arm through impact and freeze the perfect follow-through position at waist height—inside of forearm pointing away from you, thumb pointing toward the target.

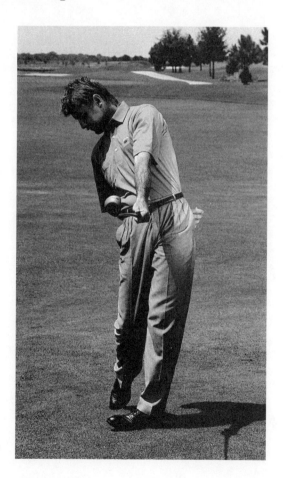

Practicing this drill will help you rotate your *left arm* correctly on the downswing.

Drill Seventeen—Tip for Good Balance

Here is a simple practice technique that will help you maintain that all-important balance from start of the swing to finish: Make a normal practice swing with the driver, and pose a perfect balanced finish for a full 2 minutes as if in front of a camera. Your weight should be almost completely on the outside of your left foot, your body facing the target with your hips level, the arms nicely relaxed and clubshaft behind you.

To enhance your balance, *pose* the finish position.

**Drill Eighteen—
Every Club
Requires the
Same Pace**

It's an extremely harmful fallacy to think that you must hit the long clubs harder—particularly the driver. This leads to overswinging, poor balance, and mishit shots of all kinds.

Here is a tip designed to ensure that you swing smoothly *through*, rather than *at*, the ball with every club in the bag: Set up to a tee shot, and in your mind's eye, see yourself swinging an 8-iron. Then try to swing as if it is that 8-iron. You'll be surprised at how even your tempo is and how solidly and accurately you drive the ball.

Setting up to a drive and seeing yourself hitting an *8-iron* shot will help you make a smooth swing.

Drill Nineteen— Stop the Shank!

A "shank" is a shot that flies dead right. Its major cause: dropping the club too far inside with the hosel leading a very open clubface. To correct this swing fault and the shank, practice as follows:

Step One. Place a second ball to the side of the ball you intend to hit. There should be 3 inches of space between them. Address the first ball in the center of the clubface.

Step Two. Swing, trying to make contact without touching the outside ball. You'll need to make contact at the clubface center or slightly toward the toe to accomplish this.

Stop the Shank Drill: Step One

Stop the Shank Drill: Step Two

**Drill Twenty—
Spot Chipping**

The simplest and most consistent way to chip is to roll the ball along the green as much like a putt as possible. However, you first need to carry the ball just a few feet onto the putting surface. Here's a practice drill that should help you accomplish your goal around the green.

Place a golf ball on the precise spot on the green where you want to land the chip shot.

Next, hit a chip and see if you can make a direct hit. When you can knock the ball off its spot consistently, with different clubs, you're ready to battle the course.

This chipping drill will enhance your *touch* around the greens.

Drill Twenty-One—Putt Like a Blind Man

One of the biggest causes of missed putts is premature movement of the head and upper body, most often caused by looking up in anxiety to see if the putt will drop into the hole.

Next time you're on the practice green, set up to some 10- to 15-foot putts as carefully as possible. Then close your eyes before you stroke them. This may feel odd on the first few strokes, but keep putting them this way. With your eyes closed, you'll eliminate that body movement because there's no reason to look up.

One final thought: Take care to line up the blade and make just as smooth a stroke as normally. If you do, you just may be surprised at how many putts you sink.

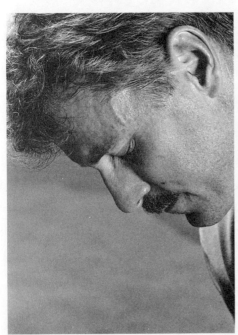

A "no-see" stroke will steady you.

Drill Twenty-Two—Practice-Putt with Your Right Hand

In Chapter Four we discussed the preferred method of stroking putts, with the right hand dominating and the left hand taking a ride. On the practice green, practice a completely right-handed stroke, keeping your left hand behind your back. Work on drawing the putter back low to the ground and pushing it through with a pistonlike motion, while keeping your right wrist flexed back even beyond impact. This ensures that the club's handle remains ahead of the clubface through impact, guaranteeing an accelerating stroke.

Practice medium-length putts (20 to 30 feet). Don't concern yourself too much with the perfect line or holding the putt. Concentrate mainly on accelerating through impact and rolling the ball the proper distance.

To build acceleration into your putting stroke, practice hitting balls *right handed*.

Drill Twenty-Three—The Short Putt Test

Sinking all of your "testers" can turn a fair score into a good one. Here's a practice-green drill to help you toughen up in this key area.

Place four lines of three balls each around the hole. The balls in each line should be 3, 4, and 5 feet out from the hole.

The catch to this drill is, if you miss at any point, you must start over. Thus, to complete the drill you must sink twelve short putts in a row. As you progress through the drill, the pressure increases because you have to keep making them to avoid starting over. That's good; facing this pressure will definitely help you during actual play.

One last point: This is a tough drill. If you haven't made twelve in a row within 30 minutes, stop and try again another day. You've still done some worthy putting practice.

Take the short putt *test* until you pass.

Drill Twenty-Four—The 30-Second Warm-up

It's always wise to get to the course at least a half hour before your tee time, so you can warm up prior to playing. But for those times when you're in a rush, here's a 30-second, two-step program that will give you a chance to get off to a good start.

1. Put your feet together and make short swings back and forth with a driver to give you a sense of swing balance (15 seconds).
2. Grip two clubs and swing them back and forth to stretch your golf muscles (15 seconds).

The Thirty-Second Warmup: Step One

The Thirty-Second Warmup: Step Two

Drill Twenty-Five—One Key Move

One sure way to quickly evolve into a good golfer is to keep your swing thoughts as simple as possible. The golfer who thinks too much about swing mechanics is the most likely to stay a hacker, or become one.

So during practice, learn to limit your thinking about the swing to just this: Remember to start your backswing by *slowly* turning the right hip and right shoulder away from the ball in unison. This gives you the best chance for a full, rhythmic backswing turn. With this, the odds of completing a sound swing and getting a high-quality result will go up dramatically.

After a while, I hope, your swing will become so automatic that it can be triggered by a "release key." The next chapter will explain how this innovative teaching system works.

Groove a simple, right-sided backswing motion in practice, and you'll never become overwhelmed by swing mechanics.

**RITSON'S
REVIEW**

- Drill One—Clap for Good Posture:
  Keep your palms parallel at address.

- Drill Two—The "Non-Milkman" Grip:
  Put pressure on the last three fingers of your left hand.

- Drill Three—One-Armed Swing:
  Swing back to the top with only your left hand and arm.

- Drill Four—Rotate Around Your Right Knee:
  Keep your right knee soft on the backswing.

- Drill Five—Left Knee Behind the Ball:
  Rotate your left knee beyond the ball.

- Drill Six—Put Weight on Your Right Heel:
  On the backswing, rotate your hips clockwise until you feel weight shift onto your right heel.

- Drill Seven—Wind It Up!:
  Turn until the butt end of the club points at a spot behind the ball.

- Drill Eight—Correcting Your Backswing Foot Fault:
  Put a clubhead under your right foot and then turn.

- Drill Nine—The Waiter's Drill:
  Hold an imaginary tray at the top of the backswing.

- Drill Ten—Check for Elbow No-Nos:
  The golf ball under your right armpit should drop out during the backswing.

- Drill Eleven—Consistent Grip Pressure—For Just 25 Cents!:
  Press the quarter with your right palm.

- Drill Twelve—Go Bowlegged Starting Down:
  Increase the distance between your knees at the start of the downswing.

- Drill Thirteen—Get "Hip" for Downswing Power:
  Push your right hip through the impact zone.

- Drill Fourteen—Be Underhanded:
  Toss an imaginary ball upward on the downswing.

- Drill Fifteen—Chase with the Right Knee:
  Rotate your right knee into your left in the hitting area.

- Drill Sixteen—Freeze the Perfect Follow-Through:
  Make a left-arm-only swing and hold the follow-through position.

- Drill Seventeen—Tip for Good Balance:
  Pose the perfect finish position for two minutes.

- Drill Eighteen—Every Club Requires the Same Pace:
  Pretend the driver is an 8-iron.

- Drill Nineteen—Stop the Shank!:
  Miss the outside ball.

- Drill Twenty—Spot Chipping:
  Knock the ball off its spot.

- Drill Twenty-One—Putt Like a Blind Man:
  Hit putts with your eyes closed to discourage looking up.

- Drill Twenty-Two—Practice-Putt with Your Right Hand:
  Feel as if you're pushing the putter into—and through—the ball with your right hand.

- Drill Twenty-Three—The Short Putt Test:
  If you miss one of twelve putts, start over.

- Drill Twenty-Four—The 30-Second Warm-up:
  1. *Swing with your feet together.* 2. *Swing two clubs.*

- Drill Twenty-Five—One Key Move:
  Trigger the backswing by slowly turning your right hip and shoulder in a clockwise direction.

10 | THE MENTAL GAME

Beyond grooving good swing mechanics, there's another game that must be mastered

I have been deeply involved with the game of golf as a player and as a teacher for nearly half a century. In that span I have observed countless championship performances by world-class players. In addition to having immense talent, these major title winners always seem to have the knack for making the great shots when they need them most.

In addition, I've watched many other tremendous golfers who, on the surface, appeared to have every bit as much ability to hit wonderful, top-quality shots; yet they never seemed to get over the hump and win the big one. Likewise, on the amateur level, I have taught thousands of golfers who did an excellent job of assimilating the mechanics. They learned a good grip, their posture and alignment were in excellent order, they swung the club on a consistent plane, and they developed sufficient acceleration for good power. Yet many of these amateurs who looked so impressive on the practice tee never seemed to perform as well as they should on the course. Often I noticed these puzzling students seemed to have a hesitancy about their swings, and they would run into problems on the course, particularly during tournaments, that really didn't show up on the practice tee during a lesson.

Of course, whenever I noticed this hesitancy in any of my students, I always made sure to try to build up their confidence, assure them they had the basics down pat, and they should just "let it rip" freely. But somehow, many students never quite seemed to fulfill their shotmaking potential. This proved very frustrating to them, and perhaps even more so to me as their instructor.

Gradually, because of these problems that went beyond the students' mechanics, I began to spend more time considering the mental side of the game. What did the champion have in his or her mental makeup that the also-ran didn't, even though the also-ran could technically drive, hit iron shots, chip, and putt just as well? Mind you, this was at a time before our modern era of golf instruction, when there were no sports psychologists to turn to for help.

I thought carefully about two particular early examples of that certain undefinable ability the champions had to perform well under duress. As a youngster I remember watching Bobby Locke, four-time British Open winner, holing a long putt during an open, even though there was a great deal of noise from a passing train just before and as he struck the putt. Almost anyone else would have stepped away from the ball in irritation in that situation, and more than likely would not stroke his best putt once he was settled in again. That little episode with Bobby Locke had stuck in my mind. Obviously, his concentration on the task at hand was somehow at a higher level than that of most other professionals.

The other example is from my own early experience. For a while, at least, I, too, had hold of something that was lifting my concentration and overall game to a different level. I was twenty years old and competing in one of my earliest professional tournaments. Somewhat surprisingly, I went on to win it. The important point I remember—though it seemed like nothing at the time—is that during the tournament I got into the habit of humming a then-popular tune to myself as I was setting up to the ball and hitting my shots. As I say, I didn't attach any importance to it. I just assumed I won that tournament because the mechanics of my game were at their peak. Never did I think there might be a connection between humming a tune and the fact that my mechanics were at their peak. And, of course, I drifted away from this little game over time as I got more and more concerned about having every point about my swing mechanics just right, and about teaching my students in the same way.

As I write this, I have now been teaching golf for some 42 years. During that time I have helped a large number of students to marked improvement. However, a teacher can never rest on his laurels and assume he is doing everything he can. Over most of this long period I now realize I may not have been giving my students everything they needed. Let me explain what I mean in a little more detail.

One Thought Is Better Than Many, But . . .

Learning all the setup and swing mechanics that we have discussed in previous chapters is not an easy task, no matter what anyone else may tell you. I don't say that to discourage you. True, some players may be lucky enough to have started playing the game while receiving excellent instruction, and have benefited from getting the fundamentals down early. Others may have played for years with many setup and swing flaws; and believe me, I understand the time and effort it takes to change them. However, anyone who aspires to a high level of play must learn all of the setup and swing mechanics that we've discussed. This process takes time and a great deal of patience. Usually, in fact, a golfer will have to take a few steps backward before any improvement starts to show. This is usually true because it's very difficult to make a free, aggressive swing while the mind is jumbled with half a dozen or more setup and swing thoughts.

However, whenever a student of mine progressed to where his mechanics were becoming ingrained, I would try to help him become more natural by asking him to focus on one particular swing thought, rather than a whole bunch of them. For one golfer, the swing thought I suggested might have been "Waggle the club slowly"; for someone else, "Rotate into your right knee." For a third person, the key thought might be, "Keep the tempo smooth as you start the downswing." This one-tip teaching definitely helped the student, but by no means did it work wonders. Something was missing.

To shorten a long story, I discovered that certain something when I met Carey Mumford, an eminent sports psychologist who specializes in helping athletes reach their peak performances. I came to meet Mumford because I had heard of his work with many golfers, both professional and amateur. I believe that what I have learned from Carey Mumford in the last few years will have a powerful effect on your ability to lower your handicap, and play more enjoyable golf, too. I would like to pay tribute here to Carey for helping me to understand the mental side of the game more clearly.

Two Types of Swing Keys

In the past, whenever I would suggest a particular swing thought for a student to focus on, in psychologist's terms I was giving him or her an *active* swing key. This means that the single thought the player has in mind while making the swing is of an actual movement he or she is trying to accomplish in the swing.

However, there is another, more effective type of key to help the golfer release the swing most effectively. This type of key is called a *passive* key. Passive keys are thoughts that trigger an activity (such as the golf swing) but which are not actually related to the swing itself. We'll talk more about these passive keys and why they are so helpful. But first, let's examine the entire thought process that's more conducive to playing good golf shots.

When you are learning the grip, setup, and swing, you must be painstakingly analytical in getting all of the mechanics correct. As you develop in the game, you constantly review your mechanics and adjust them when you've gotten off the track. Likewise, most of your thinking in playing the course is of the same analytical nature. As you tee the ball up or walk up to the ball in the fairway, there are a great many details to compute in deciding how to play the shot: The distance to your target, the lie of the ball, the direction and strength of the wind, and the hazards that threaten the shot are just a few of these factors.

This conscious planning of the shot is a crucial part of playing well. If you just assume you're about 160 yards from the hole when you're actually 175 yards away; if you fail to notice you're playing from a pronounced sidehill lie that encourages a pull or hook; or if you fail to note that the wind is against you, well, you can make the world's best swing and the ball won't finish very close to the hole. (In fact, every now and then the poor player will misjudge the conditions of the shot, then mishit the shot in just the right way so that the ball finishes close. That's really beating the odds, though.)

Now, anyone who's played the game for any length of time and is serious about his game will rarely completely overlook or misread the shot's physical characteristics. Some golfers are more fastidious and precise about analyzing shot details than others, and of course this is to their advantage. However, I have learned that there's a time and a place for analytical thinking on the golf course, and a time for another, more passive type of thought process. Later in this chapter, I will present a case study for preparing to hit a golf shot that will enlighten you on how to blend the two together to help you perform your best on every shot.

Anxiety's Debilitating Role

All of us have played at one time or another with someone who just reeks of nervousness and anxiety on the golf course. These folks seem to have forgotten that the object of the game is to hit the ball toward the hole. Instead, these players seem to get caught up in avoiding the various hazards of the course. There is no sense of freedom in their swings; they consistently steer their shots. The end result is that they hit many more poor shots per round than they should, given their basic ability to swing the club. While some golfers play with this mental handicap all the time, we all have gone through periods of greater-than-normal anxiety. At these times, every minor hazard on the course looks impossible to miss and on the green the hole looks like a thimble.

As I've learned from Mumford, all human beings are blessed with an instinctive protective system that goes into action when either our physical or mental well-being is under duress. This system acts something like a gyroscope—it keeps our systems from falling off balance in any situation.

Our gyroscope functions during times of stress by blocking any activity from occurring. And anxiety will trigger this instinctive protective system within us. Put into a golf course setting, a case of extreme anxiety, then, can actually make the golfer freeze. On the tee, he or she will stand like a statue before finally getting the club to move lurchingly away from the ball. On the greens, golfers have long been known to get the "yips." They freeze over the ball and when they finally do get the putter back, they stab at the ball, usually sending it flying way past the hole.

These are extreme cases. However, the more I learned about it, the more I realized that anxiety is really a performance-inhibiting problem, and to a degree it is a problem for all of us.

Staying in the Present

I have come to understand that many times our problem is not that our thinking about how to play a particular shot is faulty. However, most golfers are completely caught up in either the future or the past when setting up to play a golf shot. This can hurt you when it comes to actually striking the ball.

When you are figuring out the score you must shoot on the hole before you play it, your mind is operating in the *future* tense. You are plotting *what you want to happen.* Conversely, a great many golfers spend their mental energy focusing on past mistakes they may have made on the course.

I have learned through hard teaching and playing experience that when the mind is focused on either the past or the future, it is likely that anxiety will intrude on the thought process. This was a very exciting point to understand and one I had never considered before. To put this concept in a more positive light, *anxiety cannot disrupt your thought process as long as you are focused exclusively on the present.*

The key, then, in overcoming the anxiety that blocks so many of us from making our best swings on the golf course is to completely focus on the present (as opposed to the future or the past) as you are actually swinging at the ball.

Put Your Good Swings to Work

Most of the good things we do in everyday life, we perform as a matter of habit. When we climb out of bed each morning and walk straight into the kitchen to make coffee, we do it out of habit. When we get into our automobiles to go to work, we follow a pattern of movements in starting and driving the car that is also very much a habit—we don't have to think about these movements as we're doing them.

Oftentimes you hear the term *muscle memory* kicked around regarding athletic movements, and particularly regarding hitting golf shots. Well, we've come to learn that there is really no such thing as muscle memory. It is the *mind* that has a memory, and it is the mind that remembers the habits of walking and driving and automatically recalls how to do them. Likewise, it is the mind that recalls the habits you've developed in swinging the golf club.

We seem to think the term *habit* always refers to something that's negative. However, in reality habits can be good.

Once you've developed good swing habits, you must give them the freedom to work for you, rather than trying to make them work. As I've come to learn, a habit will only work if you don't give any conscious thought to it. So you see, the thought process in which we tend to analyze and prepare for the shot is *not* the thought process that's most conducive to hitting the shot. Even when you limit yourself to thinking about one aspect of your mechanics while you swing, as I used to instruct my students, you're still not giving the shot at hand your "best shot." Instead, you must learn to put your mind completely on automatic, so that you can let your natural swing go with no conscious thought directed to it. For as Mumford always says, "When a habit starts, thinking connected with that habit *stops*."

The Passive or "Release" Key

Let's now explore how to shift from our analytical thinking mode, which is so useful in learning the swing and planning our shots, to the mental state that will allow you to perform at an anxiety-free level. Do you remember how I told you I won a tournament long ago while humming a tune as I hit my shots? Well, as I look back, that was a very useful tactic (although I didn't think of it as a tactic at the time). Humming helped me because it focused my mind squarely on the present moment as I was striking the ball. And as we've learned, there's a minimum of anxiety in your system when you are truly focused on the present. So just before you actually make your swing, you need to introduce a mental key which brings you into the present but does not interrupt your setup habits.

I suggest that, rather than thinking of one or more swing keys that end up inhibiting you, learn instead to develop a *passive* key, the term I referred to earlier. For our golfing purposes, let's refer to this passive key as our "release" key, since its purpose is to help you release your golf swing with no conscious effort. According to Mumford, a release key is a thought which triggers your swing action but which does not specifically remind you about a part of your golf swing.

Your release key can be literally anything you want it to be, as long as it is not a specific command to your body such as "Drive the hips." Instead, make your release key a simple verbal trigger that has nothing to do with hitting a golf ball. Why not focus on some pleasant image as your release key? Here are some examples of release keys:

- "I love golf"
- "Merry Christmas"
- "Kalamazoo"
- "Gone fishin' "
- "Wind surfing"
- A few words from a favorite song
- "K Mart"

In a sense, I guess developing a release key for your swing is something like the development of the mantra that is used by practitioners of many Eastern religious philosophies. This mantra is their focus on which they strive to develop a heightened awareness. While the awareness you seek is not quite so far-reaching as that of the Eastern mystic, the principle involved is very much the same. You, too, are increasing your awareness of the present moment by repeating your release key as you swing.

Transition to the Release Key: A Preshot Case Study

Let's go through the process of planning, setting up to, and hitting a specific shot you might encounter during a round, so you can observe the process of moving from your usual analytical mind-set to the release key that puts you squarely in the present tense as you play the shot. At the same time, you'll be observing an example of the conscious preshot thought process you should be going through prior to every stroke. So there are two excellent benefits to this exercise.

You step up to the tee of a moderately long par four, say 400 yards. The hole doglegs slightly to the left 200 yards from the tee, and a fairway bunker guards the right side of the fairway. The green is guarded by a bunker on both sides.

In analyzing the hole before you tee up your ball, you note the following conditions:

- There's a light headwind, say 10 miles per hour.
- The flat fairway is relatively firm.
- Since the dogleg is not sharp, you can see the right side of the green by stepping over to the right side of the tee. From here you notice that the pin is on the right side, close to the right-hand bunker.

Having noted these conditions, you consider them in light of your normal tee shot and also your ability to adjust your shotmaking for the demands of the course. Let's say your normally well-hit drive covers 225 yards with a fairly high trajectory, and it flies pretty much straight. However, you're fairly confident in your ability to draw or fade your tee shots and usually will deliberately do so a few times during every round.

Now you consider where your average tee shot will leave you on this hole as it is playing today. If you hit your average tee shot 225 yards straight down the middle, it's certainly not the worst thing in the world: You'll definitely have a shot at the green. However, you realize that because the wind's against you, your normal tee shot will travel about 215 yards instead of 225. Also, because the dogleg starts left 200 yards from the tee, your down-the-middle ball will actually wind up toward the right-center of the fairway. You should note three disadvantages to this positioning of the drive:

1. The hole will play about 5 yards longer from the right-center, since it doglegs left. If it effectively plays 405 yards and your into-the-wind tee shot is 215 yards out, you're looking at a 190-yard second shot.

2. Since the pin is on the right side, close to a bunker, it will be difficult to get your approach near the hole, particularly with the long iron or fairway wood you'll need.

3. Your tee shot, if hit perfectly, will put you close to the fairway bunker. A slight push puts you in the bunker, from where you would not be able to reach the green in regulation.

Having weighed these conditions in advance, as you should, you decide it is worthwhile to hit a substantial draw from the tee. Doing so will gain you the following advantages:

1. The ball will fly a little lower and cut through the breeze better than your normal straight shot, thus getting back the 10 yards of carry you'd normally lose.

2. A draw will take better advantage of the firm fairway, giving you 10 yards extra roll in this instance. So your solid draw will get you 235 yards off the tee.

3. The 15-yard draw you envision will turn the corner and put your ball on the left-center of the fairway instead of the right-center. This cuts 5 yards off the hole's 400-yard distance. Since it will now play 395 yards and you've driven 235, you're left with only 160 to the pin—a comfortable middle iron.

4. This tee shot will leave you with an open shot to the flag—the most important advantage of all.

Before we go on, I'd like to make a point regarding this example, which is simply used to illustrate the mental preparation factors you should be considering. In this example, *everything* is weighted in favor of hitting a draw off the tee. The shape of the hole, the hazards, the pin position, the wind, and the firm fairway all point to the right-to-left shot. Also, we're assuming you have reasonable confidence in playing the draw in the first place.

Usually the factors will not be so clear-cut. Even more important, you may have been having recent trouble drawing the ball and your confidence isn't there. Confidence in playing any particular kind of shot is more important in your shotmaking decision than any physical detail of the hole. Keep that foremost in your preshot mental process. (And if you are having trouble bending the ball either way, go back and reread Chapter Three.)

Let's return to preparing for the tee shot at hand. You are still in your conscious, analytical mode. First, because you've decided to hit a draw, you'll tee the ball a fraction higher than you normally would. This automatically encourages you to swing in a slightly flatter plane that delivers the club into the ball from inside the target line, helping produce the desired drawspin.

Step behind the ball and pick the spot where you'd like the ball to finish. Next, imagine the entire trajectory of the shot, starting down the center with a substantial curve to the left and a reasonably good roll upon landing. Now, still standing behind the ball, pick a spot along the starting line of the shot. Go ahead and step up to the shot, setting up to the ball to play the power draw in the manner previously described.

Up to this point, you've remained in your analytical mental mode. Here now is the key to the mental side I have alluded to throughout this chapter. Once you have properly positioned yourself over the ball and waggled the club a few times to loosen your hands and wrists, just say your release key to yourself and immediately go ahead and swing. I believe this shift in focus to your release key will remove the anxiety and tension that is almost every golfer's bugaboo, and unlock the very best golf swing you are capable of. I don't care what your passive key is, as long as you focus on it and swing the club while you're saying it.

Turn Your Key Quickly

You see a great many golfers set up to the ball correctly, then look at their target line and back to the ball several times before actually swinging the club. However, it's not a characteristic you should emulate. I believe this practice breeds exactly the state of anxiety you are trying to overcome through the use of a release key. With this in mind, I recommend that once you have viewed the target from behind and lined yourself up, you proceed immediately into your release key and swing. I suggest this because it always seems to hold true that your first image of a shot is the clearest and most accurate one. This is true on your putts as well as your full shots. How many times have you carefully lined up a putt and then, as you stood over it, decided, "Maybe I'm lined up a tiny bit to the right"? Naturally you make a last-second adjustment, and what happens? Nine out of ten times, you pull the putt left. Case closed. Go with that first image, whether it's on a full swing, a short game shot, or a putt, and you'll be far better off in the long run.

Granted, you may want to pause for a moment before you swing in order to waggle the club, and that's okay. But I think you'll find it much easier to avoid anxiety by getting into the present as soon as possible after you're set over the ball, then pulling the trigger. Among the pros, Lee Trevino's preshot procedure is a perfect example of a setup and swing routine that involves constant motion, is quick, and allows no room for freezing. And if you have ever watched Trevino closely during play or practice, have you noticed that he's often humming something or other as he goes into his swing? Lee may not have ever studied how the mind functions or decided to create a release key, but he definitely has an intuitive grasp of how to remove anxiety by staying in the present.

As long as you give yourself enough time to set up precisely, and to move your conscious thought on to saying your release key, then go right ahead and hit the shot. Not only will you find yourself swinging more freely and hitting better shots, you'll speed up the game, too.

The true value of the release key is that it forces your mind to train itself on the present moment only, so that your golf swing habits can operate on automatic. As long as you are truly into your release key, you won't be able to think at the same time about the past (how you drove the ball out of bounds the last time you were here) or the future (the physical moves you plan to make in your swing).

Practice Your Key Out Loud

I hope you're convinced to implant a release key into your mental package. Assuming you are, I strongly recommend that you incorporate it into your game by repeating your key out loud whenever you practice. This is essentially the same advice that W. Timothy Gallwey, author of *The Inner Game of Tennis*, gives tennis players to increase their present-moment awareness. As the tennis ball hit by the opposing player crosses the net and hits the court in front of them, Gallwey tells players to yell "Bounce!" Then, after the ball bounces back up, they say "Hit!" as they swing their own racket and make contact.

The reason you should say your release key aloud is simple: If you are engaged in actually saying the words, it is impossible to think of an extraneous thought simultaneously. You can't actually say "K Mart," for instance, and think "Don't hit a duck hook!" at the same time. If you limit yourself to merely thinking of your release key rather than saying it, however, it is possible that you can fool yourself. You may be able to think you've focused on your release key, but it is also possible to allow your mind to wander onto a harmful thought, if your brain is not actually sending the message to your voice to say the words.

I know you may worry about saying your release key out loud during practice. Don't worry. Say it. You don't have to yell for the key to be effective. And no one is really going to notice. In fact, I would also like you to begin whispering your key (rather than just saying it to yourself) as you play on the course. I have been doing this myself for some four years now, since I learned this fascinating information from Carey Mumford. I can assure you from my own experience that if you integrate a release key into your routine, you'll never have a problem with your game swing consistently letting you down while your practice swing looks good.

RITSON'S REVIEW

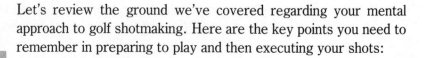

Let's review the ground we've covered regarding your mental approach to golf shotmaking. Here are the key points you need to remember in preparing to play and then executing your shots:

Before Standing Up to the Shot
- Make a complete analysis of the physical factors that will affect the upcoming shot.
- Determine the best type of shot to play, factoring in both the ideal shotmaking choice and your own shotmaking strengths and weaknesses.
- Line up the shot from a few steps behind the ball.

As You Are over the Ball
- Go into automatic by whispering your own personal release key; start the swing immediately.
- Repeat your release key out loud whenever you practice.

INDEX

A

Addressing the ball, 14, 18–21, 216–
    218. *See also* Setup
  ball position, 14, 16
  clubhead delivery and, 20–21
  distance from ball and, 20–21
  key points, summarized, 26–27
  posture, 18–21
  for putting, 112
  setup routine and, 23–25
  stance, 14–18, 26
Aiming, 21–25
  flaws in, 21–23
  key points, summarized, 27
  setup system for, 23–25
Analytical mind-set, 250–251
  transition to release key from, case
    study, 255–259
Anxiety, 251–252
  avoiding, 252–253, 257, 258

B

Backswing, 34–46
  control of club, 37, 39

for half wedge shot, 95
"in-motion" transition to
  downswing, 45–46
key points, reviewed, 57
left arm position, 42–45, 195–196,
  219
left heel, lifting on, 40–41
left knee position, 221
length of, 37, 39–40
overly flat, correcting, 199–200
reverse pivot on, correcting, 198
right arm movements, 34–39, 225,
  226
right foot fault, 24
right knee flex position, 220
right-side-controlled, 46
rotation power in, 34–37, 40
swaying off ball on, correcting,
  196–197
too upright, correcting, 201
Balance, maintaining, 54, 165, 234
Ball position
  for driver, 14–16
  for full shots, 14–16
Ballesteros, Seve, 29, 120
Bounce, 122
Bunker(s), 98, 119–120

Bunker shots
    club selection, 121–122
    downhill bunker shot, 135–136
    fairway bunker techniques, 137–
      141
    greenside bunker techniques, 122–
      127, 141
    from hard sand, 129–131
    ice cream scoop shot, 131–134
    margin for error in, 127, 129
    for special situations, 129–
      141
    uphill lie under the lip, 137
    wood shot, 184–187

C

Chipping, 106–109, 116–117
    club selection, 108
    key factors, reviewed, 116–117
    practice drill, 237
    stance, 109
    stroke, 109
    techniques, 108–109
    in wind, 157
Club(s). *See* Club selection; Irons;
    Lofted wedge; Pitching wedge;
    Putter; Sand wedge; Woods
Club selection
    for chipping, 108
    for fairway bunker shots, 139,
      140
    for hardpan shots, 183
    for light rough, 174
    for medium or deep rough, 172
    for pitch-and-run, 103–104
    for sand trap shots, 121–122, 139,
      140
    windy weather conditions and, 145,
      146–148
"Cuppy" fairway lie, 164, 189,

D

"Dagger drill," 92
Divot, extricating ball from, 162–164,
    189
Down-target view, 18
Downhill lie, 164–165, 167, 189
    bunker shot, 135–136
Downswing
    for full pitch wedge, 90–92
    for half wedge shots, 95–98
    hip clearance, 230
    "in-motion" transition to,
      45–46
    keeping clubhead away from ball on,
      46, 48–50
    key points, reviewed, 57
    left leg on, 229
    left-side-controlled, 46, 48–50
    lower-body lunge, correcting, 203–
      204
    maximum clubhead speed and
      consistency on, 50–52
    outside-in swing path, correcting,
      204
    release, correcting, 212
    right knee movement, 232
    right-side movement, practicing,
      231
Draw, hitting. *See* Power draw
Drills, 215–244
    Be Underhanded, 231, 245
    Chase with Right Knee, 232, 245
    Check for Elbow No-Nos, 226,
      244
    Clap One for Good Posture, 216–
      218, 244
    Consistent Grip Pressure—
      Twenty-Five Cent Lesson, 227–
      228, 244
    Correcting Your Backswing Foot
      Fault, 224, 244

Every Club Requires the Same Pace, 235, 245

Freeze the Perfect Follow-Through, 233, 245

Get "Hip" for Downswing Power, 230, 244

Go Bowlegged Starting Down, 229, 244

key points, summarized, 244–245

Left Knee Behind Ball, 221, 244

"Non-Milkman" Grip Drill, 218, 244

One Key Move, 242, 245

One-Armed Swing, 219, 244

Practice-Putt with Your Right Hand, 239, 245

Put Weight on Your Right Heel, 222, 244

Putt Like a Blind Man, 238, 245

Rotate Around Your Right Knee, 220, 244

Short-Putt Test, 240, 245

Spot Chipping, 237, 245

Stop the Shank, 236, 245

30-Second Warm-up, 241, 245

Tip for Good Balance, 234, 245

Waiter's Drill, 225, 244

Wind It Up, 223, 244

Driver, 235

draw shot with (see Power draw)

fade shot with (see Power fade)

stance for, 14–16

"sweeping" action for, 16

Duck hook, correcting, 212

E

8-iron, 103–104, 109

Elbow(s)

left, on backswing, 195–196

right, on backswing, 193–194

F

Fade, hitting. See Power fade

Fairway

power draw and, 69–71

power fade and, 77–78

Fairway bunker shots, 137, 139–140

wood shot, 184–187

Feel, for shots, 95

Finish position, posing, 54–55, 58, 234, 245

5-iron, 17, 140, 163–164, 169, 187

Flip shot, greenside, 98–102

key factors, reviewed, 116

practicing, 101–102

swing, 100–101

Floyd, Ray, 30–31

Focusing on present moment, 252–253, 254–255, 258–259

release key and, 254–255, 257, 258–259

Follow-through, 53–56

drill, 233

finish position, 54–55, 58, 234, 245

maintaining balance in, 54, 234

key points, reviewed, 58

Reverse C, correcting, 210–211

Foot position. See Stance

4-iron, 139, 163–164, 177

Full wedge pitch, 88–93, 116

control of, 92

key factors, reviewed, 116

setup, 88–90

swing, 90–92

G

Gallwey, W. Timothy, 259

Golf swing. See Swing

Greenside bunkers. See Bunker(s)

Greenside bunker shots, 119–120

Greenside bunker shots (*cont.*)
    stance, 123, 125
    swing, 125–127
    techniques, basic, 122–127, 141
Greenside chipping. *See* Chipping
Greenside flip shot, 98–102
    key factors, reviewed, 116
    practicing, 101–102
    swing, 100–101
Greenside rough. *See* Rough:
    greenside
Grip
    consistent pressure on, practicing,
        227–228
    correct, keys to, 3–14
    for greenside bunker shots, 125
    interlocking, 3–4
    key points, summarized, 26
    left-hand position, 6–7, 9
    "milking," preventing, 12–13, 218
    overlapping, 2, 8
    palms-parallel position, 4–5
    for power draw, 75
    for power fade, 82
    pressure on, 3, 10–12, 227–228
    for putting, 111–112
    right-hand position, 7–9
    "strong," 13–14
    too upright swing and, 201
    "weak," 13–14

H

Habits, 253
Half wedge shot, 93–98
    key factors, reviewed, 116
    sand wedge for, 93–94
    setup, 94–95
    swing, 95–98
Hardpan, shot off, 183
Head movement, 25, 52–53
Hips, 14, 25, 37

Hook, 22, 68
    outside-in swing plane and,
        206
    around trees, 174, 177

I

Ice cream scoop shot, 131–134
Impact zone, 50–53
    key points, reviewed, 57–58
Interlocking grip, 2, 3, 4, 8
Iron play, in wind, 152–157
Irons, 94, 120
    3-iron, 16, 17
    4-iron, 139, 163–164, 177
    5-iron, 17, 140, 163–164, 169,
        187
    6-iron, 109, 140
    7-iron, 103, 109, 152, 162, 177
    8-iron, 103–104, 109
    9-iron, 103–104, 109

J

Jones, Bobby, 29

K

Kite, Tom, 3, 30
Knee flex, 19, 20, 34–35, 36
    correcting loss of, 208–209
    maintaining, practice drill, 220,
        244

L

Left-handed recovery shot, 187–188
Locke, Bobby, 248
Lofted wedge, 122

M

Mental attitude, 191. *See also* Mental
    game
  to greenside chip shot, 107–108
  toward wind play, 144–145, 159
Mental game, 247–260
  active swing keys, 249–250
  focusing on present moment, 252–
    253, 254–255, 258–259
  key points, reviewed, 260
  release key, 250, 251, 254–260
Mumford, Carey, 250, 251, 253,
    259
Muscle memory, 253

N

Nicklaus, Jack, 3, 39–40
9-iron, 103–104, 109
Norman, Greg, 40

O

Overlap grip, 2, 8

P

Passive key. *See* Release key
Pitch-and-run, 102–106, 116
  address position, 104
  club selection for, 103–104
  key factors, reviewed, 116
  situations calling for, 103
  swing, 104
Pitching wedge, 105, 109
  versus sand wedge, 88, 94, 121
  stance for, 17
Player, Gary, 120
Power draw, 67–77

clubhead and body alignment for,
    72–75, 76
  grip for, 75
  high-teed ball for, 71–73
  key points, reviewed, 85
  practicing, 76–77
  technique, 71–77
  when to play, 69–71
Power fade, 77–84
  grip for, 82
  key points, reviewed, 85
  low-teed ball for, 80–81
  practicing, 84
  setup for, 82
  swing, 82–83
  when to use, 77–80
Practice drills. *See* Drills
Preshot routine. *See* Setup
Preswing waggles, 30–31
Punch shot
  into-the-wind, 152–154
  with wind at back, 154–155
Purtzer, Tom, 40
Putter, 110
Putting, 109–115, 117
  address position, 11
  grip, 111–112
  key factors, reviewed, 117
  mental preparation for, 110
  practice drills, 238, 239, 240
  setup for, 111–112
  short putt test drill, 240
  stroke, 111, 112–115
  in wind, 157–158
Putting green, assessing, 110–111

R

Release key (passive key), 242, 250,
    251, 254–260
  function of, 254–255
  practicing out loud, 259

Release key (passive key) (*cont.*)
  transition to, preshot case study,
    255–259
Reverse C problem, correcting, 210
Rodriguez, Chi Chi, 120
Rotation power
  in backswing, developing, 34–37,
    40
  at impact, 51–52
Rough
  greenside, playing from, 98–102
  light, playing from, 174
  medium or deep, playing from, 172,
    174

S

Sand shots, 119–140. *See also*
    Fairway bunker shots; Greenside
    bunker shots
Sand wedge, 88, 94, 99
  correct, selecting, 121–123
  for greenside flipping, 99
  half wedge shot with, 94
  versus pitching wedge, 88, 94, 121
Scoop technique. *See* Ice cream scoop
    shot
Setup, 1–27. *See also* Addressing the
    ball
  consistent routine for, 23–25
  for half wedge shot, 94–95
  key points, summarized, 26–27
  for power draw, 71–75, 77
  for power fade, 82
  use of release key, 257–258 (*see
    also* Mental game)
7-iron, 103, 109, 152, 162, 177
Shank
  defined, 236
  stopping, drill for, 236
Short game, 87–117

defined, 87
outer limit of, 88
in windy conditions, 157–158, 159
Shoulder(s), 25
  address posture, 25
  on backswing, 36–38
  on downswing, 53, 202
Sidehill lie
  with ball above feet, 167, 169, 189
  with ball below feet, 169, 189
6-iron, 109, 140
Skip shot, 183–184
Slice, 68, 76
  right-side domination as cause of,
    46
  around trees, 177–178
Snead, Sam, 29
Stance, 14–18
  club length and 14, 16–17
  for driver, 14, 16
  for irons, 16–17
  key points, summarized, 26
  and length of club, 14
  for pitching wedge shot, 17
  for standard full shots, 14–18
  sweep in relation to, 26
  weight distribution and, 16–18
  for woods, 16
Stewart, Payne, 29
Swing, 29–65. *See also* Backswing;
    Downswing; Follow-through;
    Swing faults, and cures;
    Takeaway
  backswing, 34–46, 57
  controlled, 30
  downswing, 46–53, 57
  erratic, 30
  follow-through, 53–56, 58
  impact zone, 50–53, 57–58
  for power draw, 75–77
  release key for, 242, 250, 251,
    254–260

Swing (*cont.*)
  setup position and, 1
  simplifying thoughts about, 242
  smooth, practice technique for, 235
  takeaway, 31, 32–33, 57
  transition, 45–46
  waggle as precursor to, 30–31, 57
Swing faults, and cures, 191–213
  flying right elbow, on backswing,
    193–194
  inside-out swing plane, 206
  lower body lunge, on downswing,
    203–204
  outside-in swing plane, on
    downswing, 204
  overly flat swing plane, on
    backswing, 199–200
  Reverse C, 210–211
  reverse pivot, on backswing, 198
  reviewed, 213
  right-shoulder dip, on downswing,
    202
  severely bent left elbow, on
    backswing, 195–196
  standing up on shot, 208
  swaying off the ball, on backswing,
    196–197
  swing too upright, on backswing,
    201
  wrong release, 212
Swing keys
  active, 249–250
  passive, 250, 251, 254–260

T

Takeaway, 31, 32–33, 37
  for full pitch wedge, 90
  key points, reviewed, 57
3-iron, 16, 17
Tight lie, 169, 172, 189

"Tray" position, 35
Trees
  and left-handed recovery shot,
    187–188
  low hook around, 174, 177
  shot over, 180
  shot under branch, 178, 180
  slice around, 177–178
Trevino, Lee, 258
Trouble shot techniques, 161–189
Turns, athletic, 223

U

Uphill lie, 167, 189
Uphill sand shots, 137–138

W

Waggle, preswing, 30–31, 57
Warm-up, thirty-second, 241
Water hazards, skip shot for, 183–
  184
Wedge. *See* Lofted wedge; Pitching
  wedge; Sand wedge
Wedge shots. *See* Full wedge pitch;
  Half wedge shot
Weight distribution, 16, 17, 19–20,
  34, 37, 232
  for chip shot, 109
  drill, 222
  on impact with ball, 50
Wind factors, 143–159. *See also*
    Windy-weather playing strategies
  area of country and, 144
  gauging accurately, 145–146
  mental attitude toward, 144–
    145
Windy-weather playing strategies,
  148–158, 159

Windy-weather playing strategies
    (*cont.*)
  crosswind driving strategy, 150,
    152, 155, 157
  downwind punch, 154–155
  iron play, 152–157
  key points, reviewed, 159
  pitch-and-run shot, 103
  playing into wind, 148–149, 152–
    154
  playing with the wind, 150, 154–
    155
  power draw, 70, 71
  power fade, 79–80
  punch shot, 152–154
Women golfers, 37
Woods. *See also* Driver
  for fairway bunker play, 184–
    187
  lofted, for deep rough, 172,
    174
  "nipping" action for, 16
  stance for, 16
Wrist(s)
  left, 42, 45, 50
  right, 45, 50–51, 83–84

ABOUT
THE AUTHORS

Phil Ritson is a veteran golf instructor whom *GOLF* Magazine recently named one of the seven top teachers in the United States.

Ritson, whose simple teaching philosophy is "Eliminate all the unnecessary moving parts in the swing," has given over 130,000 lessons to pros, amateurs, and fellow teachers, including superstar senior professional Gary Player, Notre Dame football coach Lou Holtz, and renowned golf instructor David Leadbetter.

A former playing professional and winner of the prestigious South African Dunlop Masters Championship, Ritson does color golf commentary for television and radio.

Ritson's videos, *Golf Your Way* and *Encyclopedia of Golf,* were given top marks by *GOLF* Magazine and are currently high on the bestseller list.

Ritson, who is the former golf director at Walt Disney World, currently operates golf schools at the Windermere Golf Club in Orlando, Florida, and at Pawleys Plantation in Pawley's Island, South Carolina.

When not teaching in the United States, Ritson travels the world giving individual lessons and group seminars to golfers of all ages and handicaps.

John Andrisani is the senior editor of instruction at *GOLF* Magazine and a former assistant editor of Britain's *Golf Illustrated* magazine.

Andrisani has coauthored three major instruction books with the game's top tour pros: *Learning Golf: The Lyle Way,* with Sandy Lyle; *Natural Golf,* with Seve Ballesteros; and *101 Supershots,* with Chi Chi Rodriguez. He is also the coauthor of *The Golf Doctor* and of the book *Hit it Hard!* with power hitter Mike Dunaway.

A former holder of the American Golf Writers' Championship, Andrisani plays off a 4-handicap at Lake Nona Golf Club in Orlando, Florida.

Ken Lewis, who trained at England's Southend School of Art, is recognized as one of the world's leading illustrators of the golf swing.

His work has appeared in several major books and golf publications, including *GOLF* Magazine and *Golf World* magazine.